Going To The Moors

Red grouse: The Morning Call (*1911*), *a watercolour by Archibald Thorburn* (*1860–1935*)

Going To The Moors

RONALD EDEN

JOHN MURRAY
LONDON

© Ronald Eden 1979

First published 1979 by
John Murray (Publishers) Ltd
50 Albermarle Street, London W1X 4BD

Printed in Great Britain by
Fletcher & Son Ltd, Norwich

Designed by Peter Campbell

British Library Cataloguing in Publication Data

Eden, Ronald
   Going to the moors
     1. Grouse shooting – Social aspects – Scotland
     I. Title
   394'.3   SK325.G7

  ISBN 0–7195–3631–6

Contents

FOR ROSEMARY

Illustrations

CAMEOS

ACKNOWLEDGEMENTS

Among those who have made valuable suggestions while I have been writing this book I should like to thank particularly Mrs Monica Clough, Miss Anne Harrel and Mrs Carola Shepherd. Major B. D. M. Booth and the Tryon Gallery, London, have generously assisted with the selection of illustrations. I am indebted also to Miss Frances Dimond, Curator, Photograph Collection, Royal Archives, Windsor; and to Mrs Claudia Lindquist for picture research. Finally, I should like to record my appreciation of the courtesy of the staffs of the London Library, the National Library of Scotland, the Scottish Record Office and the Library of the University of Stirling.

Grateful acknowledgement is also given to Faber & Faber Ltd for permission to use extracts from *The Twelfth* by J. K. Stanford.

SOURCES OF ILLUSTRATIONS

Her Majesty The Queen: plates 7, 12, 46, 47, 58, 63
G. L. Carlisle Esq, Goring: plates 30, 31, 55, 61
Eric Hosking Esq, FRPS, London: plates 27, 29
Keyser Gallery, Cirencester: plate 41
National Museum of Antiquities of Scotland (Country Life Archive), Edinburgh, and Sir John Gilmour, Bt., Leven, Fife: plates 56, 75, 76
Punch Publications Ltd, London: plates 52, 66, 67, 78, 86
Radio Times Hulton Picture Library, London: plates 3, 4, 8, 9, 10, 11, 14, 20, 22, 42, 48, 49, 57, 59, 62, 69, 72, 89
Harry Smith Collection, Rettendon, Chelmsford: plate 28
Thorburn Museum, Dobwalls, Cornwall, and the Tryon Gallery Ltd, London: plates 34, 82
Tryon Gallery Ltd, London: frontispiece and plates 2, 6, 21, 33, 35, 36, 37, 38, 39, 50, 51, 70, 71, 77, 79, 80, 81, 83, 84, 93
Walker Art Gallery, Liverpool: plates 44, 64

Illustrations on the half-title page and on pages 15, 37, 49 and 119 are from *The Graphic* (13 September 1879) and are reproduced by permission of the Radio Times Hulton Picture Library. Those on pages 99, 131, 133, 186, 187, 189, 191 are from the author's collection.

Born to the Hill

The day before I was born my mother went pigeon shooting. To the horrified plea of the gamekeeper that she should not be so rash she said that if I arrived I could be placed in the game bag.

With such parentage it was natural that I should pursue field sports at an early age, and I had killed my first grouse and my first stag by the age of nine. Later, as an undergraduate at Oxford, second-hand bookshops revealed to me the huge and entrancing Victorian literature centred on Scottish sport. Those were the days when a signed copy of Charles St John's *Wild Sports and Natural History of the Highlands*, or William Scrope's *Days of Deer-Stalking*, could be had for less than a pound. The volumes of the Badminton Library, the monographs of the Fur and Feather Series, together with the works of Gathorne-Hardy, Innes Shand, Bromley Davenport, Peel and a score of other writers, formed the nucleus of a library of Scottish sport which I began to accumulate.

The uniqueness and romantic mystique of the grouse derive in great part from the fact that it is indigenous only in the British Isles. Even within these islands attempts to introduce the red grouse, *Lagopus lagopus scoticus*, as distinct from the black grouse and the ptarmigan, into districts outside its natural range have met with failure. Scotland is its traditional home, and it is of Scotland that I write, but it occurs more or less plentifully in the north of England, Wales, Shropshire and the hills of Ireland. When introduced to the Shetlands, Surrey, Norfolk, Suffolk and Exmoor it has either not survived or failed to thrive. Foreign countries have tried to establish it—in Sweden near Gothenburg, on high moorland on the borders of Germany and Belgium and in New Zealand—but it has soon perished. To naturalists an enigma, to sportsmen a bird unmatched in allure, to left-wing politicians a metaphoric rod to castigate the Establishment, to newspaper editors one of the birds whose fortunes at birth, mating time and death are good copy; such is the red grouse, and so it has been for 150 years.

I say something of the natural history of the grouse in a later chapter, but it is a surprising fact that in spite of the large literature it has generated, concerned both with the life it leads and the sport it gives, social histories of Scotland have alluded only briefly to the social and economic aspects of the sporting boom. Much has been written of the sheep clearances but no history has been written of the boom that succeeded those clearances. A work of scholarship is needed to analyse the effect on Highland society and on the Highland economy wrought by the shooting and fishing mania, for although it was of less importance than the coming of the sheep, nevertheless it was crucial in helping to fill a chasm in the economy when the slump in sheep came.

This book does not pretend to be a definitive work, nor indeed is it based on very original scholarship, but I hope that I have highlighted the principal causes and effects of the passion for Highland sports and, at the same time, brought back to life the colourful panorama that constituted this aspect of the Victorian scene. My sources are composed chiefly of the books and magazine articles of the period on sport and travel, memoirs and fiction. While the historian must approach the novel in his search for truth with some diffidence, at the same time he must take pains to recognise that fiction can sometimes illuminate the truth in a manner that factual narrative cannot. Thomas Jeans's *The Tommiebeg Shootings* and the satirical references to sport which I have drawn on from Anthony Trollope's Palliser novels have this quality.

I conceived the idea of writing this book twenty years ago, but other occupations precluded me from pursuing it until recently. Then, a chain of events gave me more time and spurred me on. A few years ago I inherited a grouse moor. Many people come to shoot it from different countries—the United States, Belgium, Finland, France, Germany, Italy—and when I show my guests the old family game books at Cromlix, which comprise a complete record of the moor from 1856, they immediately begin to be curious as to the history of grouse-shooting. When did it start? When did driving begin to supersede dogging? How did one get to Scotland? What were the lodges like? They ask these and many other questions. I hope this book will answer some of their questions, and stimulate further the curiosity of that great band of international sportsmen which seeks its relaxation in the heather.

Ronald Eden
August 1978

PART ONE

Earliest Times

1 [overleaf] *The red grouse: an engraving by Thomas Bewick from his* History of British Birds (*1826*)
  For cameo opposite and others following see List of Illustrations

2 Gentlemen Grouse-Shooting on the Moors *by Philip Reinagle* (*1749–1833*)

CHAPTER I

Scotland Discovered

Luncheon

Seeing Scotland, Madam, is only seeing
a worse England. *Dr Samuel Johnson, 1778*

Before the 18th century there was little to draw a foreigner to Scotland in search of
pleasure. Natural history or impressive scenery were not subjects of curiosity, and
travel records that survive usually reflect missions of a diplomatic or military
nature. Notable exceptions among the few hardy, inquisitive or eccentric souls
who went to Scotland with no business purpose in mind were Ben Jonson, who
walked there in 1618 at the age of forty-five, and John Taylor the water poet, who
went in the same year, without a penny in his pocket. If travellers went to
Scotland specifically for sport before the 18th century only one left behind an
account of his experiences. Richard Franck, a trooper in Cromwell's army in 1650
was excited by the opportunities for an angler, and returned in that peaceful guise
six years later. His *Northern Memoirs* (1658) displayed an enthusiasm for the
natural scenery unique among early writers, and though his tapered line became
entangled among the weeds of theology he gave some vivid pictures of his wander-
ings. The Clyde was then a famous river for salmon and trout, and finding the
English Commandant of Dumbarton Castle a brother angler Franck went fishing
with him, using such esoteric baits as a locust and a legless grasshopper. But
further north he found the wildness depressing so that 'the very thought of
England sweetens my apprehensions, that possibly e're long I may taste of a
southern salad: However, this I'll say in the honour of Scotland, that cold and
hunger are inseparable companions, but their linens are fresh; and were not their
beds so short they would serve well enough for weary travellers.'

The remoteness of Scotland from England was accentuated by its traditional
alliance with France. Scotland was not of a mind to look to England for ideas; an
insularity typified by Calvinism expressed in the 17th century, by the refusal
to co-operate with England unless England would adopt the Scots form of religion.

Under these circumstances it was not surprising that the common English
impression of Scotland should be an austere one. At the beginning of the 18th

century a current English proverb held that if Cain had been a Scotsman God would have changed his punishment and, instead of banishing him, would have condemned him to remain at home. If the Frenchman had wished to judge the fairness of the proverb he would have done as well to consult a fellow countryman as to consult an Englishman, such was the latter's ignorance of his northern neighbours. The belief of Smollett's Tabitha Bramble that Scotland could only be reached by sea was shared in fact as well as in fiction.

After the Forty-five the final demise of the Jacobite cause and the system of roads which the English army of occupation built at last made a journey to the Highlands of Scotland a safe and practical venture. At the same time interest in Scotland was stimulated by the achievements which in so many spheres of activity that nation was now attaining. While Scottish regiments fought in the Seven Years War against France and added pride to the British army, Scotland itself was achieving prosperity. Trade grew and the ports of Glasgow and Leith flourished, the former handling more than half the tobacco brought into Britain. The manufacture of iron and steel, linen and woollens thrived, and the literati of Edinburgh earned for that city the title of the Athens of the North. Little later than the middle of the century Voltaire was able to remark that from Scotland emanated the rules of taste in all the arts, from the epic poem to gardening.

One of the first English writers to express in a detailed and analytical way the beauties of nature was William Gilpin, and in both his books and in his paintings he did much to popularise the idea of picturesque beauty. For him the visible boundaries of property, such as hedges or stone dykes which divided open country, were a deformity in landscape. In Scotland these intersections were rarely met with; all was unbounded, and vast tracts of land were entirely in a state of nature. Ceres, Triptolemus and all the worthies who introduced corn and tillage deserved unquestionably the thanks of mankind, but at the same time it was necessary to acknowledge that they had miserably scratched and injured the face of the globe. So far as Scotland was concerned the face of nature was certainly coarse, but it was a comely face, and though the barren features of the landscape had no great share of sweetness and beauty it was wildly graceful and expressive. The pervasiveness of Gilpin's philosophy is illustrated by an anecdote told by Lockhart in his life of Scott. 'Look this way Mrs Laidlaw,' said Tom Purdie, Sir Walter Scott's gamekeeper to the factor's wife, 'and I'll show you what the gentlefolk likes. See ye there now the sun glinting on Melrose Abbey? It's no aw bright, nor it's no aw shadows neither, but just a bit screed o' light—and a bit daud o' dark yonder like and that's what they ca' picturesque, and, indeed, it maun be confessed it is unco bonnie to look at!'

3 *Engraving of a pioneer sportsman advancing to the point in the Highlands. Style of dress and mode of shooting made such compositions attractive to artists*

The most dramatic of Scott's successes in the new-found romance of landscape was 'The Lady of the Lake'. So vivid was the poem that 20,000 copies were sold within a few months. The shores of Loch Katrine, hitherto comparatively un-known, were crowded with visitors, and a boatman on Loch Lomond was so incensed by the fall in demand for his services that he said he would drown Scott if he could lay his hands on him. The glamour of Scottish scenery and the vivid history of Scotland's heroic and turbulent past were delineated by a master of historical fiction who knew what the public wanted. The rich had their Grand Tour of Europe, but now the middle-class literati had their own tour, based on the events and places of Scott's prose and poetry.

Without these early tourists there would have been little incentive to improve roads, inns, canals and other facilities necessary for sportsmen as well as sightseers, but the recreation of field sports in Scotland was being written about by the 18th century; Thomas Pennant, who travelled to Scotland in 1769 and 1772, set down in three volumes many observations on the natural history of the country and described some early attempts at game preservation. Birds of prey were pro-scribed, and their destruction was encouraged by the reward of half a crown for

4 A primitive impression of stern Caledonia

an eagle, and a shilling for a hawk or a hooded crow. Fifty years earlier Captain Edward Burt, who carried out administrative duties in the town of Inverness under General Wade, found field sports both a means of using his leisure and of varying his diet. He fed well, he tells us, on things that would have been esteemed rarities in London, such as fresh salmon and trout, partridges, grouse, hares, duck, woodcock and snipe. The cheapness of game was due to its abundance in the neighbourhood and the magistrates turned a blind eye to poachers; there was plenty for everybody and if poachers had not been allowed to bring game to the market there would have been none for the magistrates to buy. Transportation was, by law, the penalty for taking salmon fry, but the river was so full of them that nobody minded the children taking them with a crooked pin.

The stalking of red and roe deer had little appeal for Burt, although he made a few expeditions, and besides the fact that stalking was not considered a worthy sport for gentlemen the discomfort of spending several nights consecutively out on the hills made his reluctance understandable. But the shooting of feathered game he enthused over, particularly the woodcock-shooting in the coverts around Culloden House, '. . . the best spot for cock-shooting that I ever knew'.

Colonel Thomas Thornton is the earliest example of the wealthy Englishman

5 *Portrait of Colonel Thomas Thornton (1757–1823) by Philip Reinagle. Just as Scott's writings opened the eyes of the tourist to the beauty of the Highlands, so Thornton's* Sporting Tour (*1804*) *helped beckon the sportsman*

who made the Scottish moors and lochs his autumn playground. He was born in 1757 and his knowledge of Scotland dated from the age of fourteen when he was a student at Glasgow University. With a large fortune at his disposal and enthusiasm for field sports fostered at Glasgow, Thornton set about making his family home at Thornville Royal in Yorkshire the greatest sporting centre in the realm. He kept a pack of fox-hounds, raced both on horse and on foot, fished, hawked and shot. *A Sporting Tour through the northern parts of England and great part of the Highlands of Scotland* is in fact, though not by the author's admission, a composite account of several visits he paid to the north during the 1780s. The book appeared in print in 1804, and an edition by Sir Herbert Maxwell, with Garrard's engravings and coloured plates by G. E. Lodge, was published in 1896. No great literary merit can be claimed for the book, but the conveyance of hawks, dogs and the general wherewithal to entertain many guests necessitated planning in a hospitable but wild country, and no one else bequeathed to posterity such a full and clear description of ways of sport which are now past history.

Thornton evidently derived much of his knowledge of Scotland from Thomas Pennant. When Thornton sought topographical descriptions as padding for his own book he hacked and hewed at Pennant's work in a shameless feat of plagiarism. He planned his expeditions from a careful study of Pennant, whose recordings of detail were immensely valuable to the traveller, were he sportsman or otherwise. Loch Leven, Pennant told him, was already celebrated for its pink-fleshed trout; and in Loch Tay there were trout of 30 lb in weight, besides perch, eels, salmon and char. All the game birds we know today were represented except the capercailzie, which had become extinct in the 1780s, the present stock being descended from birds imported from Sweden in 1837 and 1838 by Lord Breadalbane. There were fellow sportsmen to visit such as the Duke of Gordon who still kept up the practice of falconry and had several hawks 'of the peregrine and gentle falcon species, which breed in the rocks of Glenmore'. So the Colonel made his plans, not like Pennant who relates that, 'struck . . . with the reflection of having never seen Scotland, I instantly ordered my baggage to be got ready, and in a reasonable time found myself on the banks of the Tweed', but with a great expedition, backed by his wealth and the resources of his sporting establishment.

The expedition assembled at Thornville at the end of May. Thornton ordered two portable fishing boats, one for himself and one for his friend Mr Parkhurst who accompanied him, a portable kitchen stove, guns, dogs, nets, oatmeal, beans and other stores, most of which were loaded on a cutter at Hull to sail for Forres, the nearest port to Raits on Speyside, where he had rented a house. With the crew of captain and two sailors there went his housekeeper, falconer, wagoner, groom

6 *Colonel Thornton with his celebrated pointers Juno and Pluto, painted by Sawrey Gilpin, R.A.* (*1733–1807*)

and boy. He and Parkhurst, together with the painter George Garrard, travelled by land. Garrard, a young pupil of Sawrey Gilpin the animal painter, William Gilpin's brother, had been recommended to Thornton as a suitable artist to depict for him sporting scenes and picturesque views, and was one of several sporting artists whom Thornton patronised generously, among them Sawrey Gilpin himself and the elder Reinagle.

The journey to Scotland was leisurely. As they meandered along wherever good fishing took them Garrard painted picturesque views and Thornton set down his notes on the scenery in the approved literary style. At Morpeth Thornton visited King, a dog-breaker, who had supplied him with setters in his Glasgow years, and it would be interesting to know what demand there was for sporting dogs at that time. In mid-June they reached Edinburgh where more equipment and stores were bought and loaded on wagons for dispatch to Raits. There were two chests of biscuits, Cheshire and Gloucester cheeses, Yorkshire hams, reindeer and other tongues, 70 lb of gunpowder and shot, fishing rods and tackle, guncases and plaids. Such purchases seem superfluous in view of the cargo of similar goods shipped on the cutter, and perhaps were made some other year for another expedition. Old friends were visited at Edinburgh and Glasgow, where Thornton watched golf being played on the green, a game he slightingly referred to as 'a wholesome exercise for those who do not think such gentle sports too trivial for men . . .'. At last, on 10 July, the party reached Raits. The servants had already arrived after an unpleasant seaborne trip from Hull to Forres during which their ship had sprung a leak and reached harbour only under the escort of a fishing smack. It had taken no less than forty-nine carts to convey the baggage overland, and even then the two fishing boats had to wait for a return journey. These were carried on a kind of sledge drawn by four horses.

In addition to shooting, the expedition afforded Thornton an opportunity for falconry, a sport which had already suffered decline through the increase of enclosures. Falconry could be practised more easily in Scotland than in England (as it can be now) because of the large open areas that could be ranged over. At that time the proprietors of a Highland county could almost be counted on the fingers of one hand and hill land was of such little value that boundaries were ill defined. So far as his firearms were concerned, Thornton's armoury reflected his taste for grandeur. The flintlock gun in use at this time was usually single-barrelled; double-barrelled guns only came into fashion at the beginning of the 19th century after Joseph Manton's improvements. Yet Thornton had not only double barrels but also a seven-barrelled gun and one monster double seven-barrel. The complete gun with all fourteen barrels weighed 11 lb 8 oz. Nevertheless, although he used a double-barrelled gun in Scotland he was not fond of it. On 15 September he wrote, 'I gave up my double barrel gun for the season; and here I must remark that I look upon all double barrels as trifles rather nick nacks than useful.' His favourite single Flints were named Death and Destruction.

The fact that the first day on the moors was evidently 6 August demands comment. By an Act of Parliament in 1773 the dates between which grouse might be killed, namely 12 August and 10 December, were laid down but not closely adhered to for some time. On the day in question reveille was at 4.30, and the party set off for Glen Einich at eight o'clock. The Spey was unfordable and they made a diversion to Ruthven ferry, which added four miles to the journey. By ten o'clock the temperature was 84°F, and at noon they reached the snowline, where, in a convenient drift, they buried their supplies of champagne, lime, shrub,*

* A drink prepared from the juice of orange or lemon or other fruit, sugar and spirit, usually rum.

porter,* etc., to await their return. A grouse and ptarmigan which had been shot over the pointers on the way up were also left for the servants to prepare. When the summit of Carn Ban More was reached the whole party, said Thornton, was struck equally with admiration and horror. Imagine, he said, a mountain towering at least 18,000 ft above you, and a steep precipice of 13,000 ft below! As Carn Ban is 3,443 ft in height and Braeriach, the highest mountain of the group, less than a thousand feet higher, it would seem that an extra nought crept into his figures.

Most of the party descended the glen to Loch Einich but Thornton, who had hurt his leg a few days before, stayed on the top to shoot ptarmigan. After five hours his exhausted friends returned, among them Captain Waller, to whom was pointed out a near-by ptarmigan crouching on the ground. He shot it, not knowing that it was one of Thornton's own birds placed in a lifelike position, but innocent of the ruse his spirits were revived successfully.

There followed what must have been a very welcome dinner: '. . . the chief dish consisted of two brace and a half of ptarmigans and a moorcock, a quarter of a pound of butter, some slices of Yorkshire smoked ham, and a reindeer's tongue; with some sweet herbs, pepper, etc., prepared by the housekeeper at Raits. These, with a due proportion of water, made each of us a plate of very strong soup, which was relished with a keenness of appetite that none but those who have been at Glen Einich can experience.' All this was washed down with the snow-cooled champagne and sherbet with the toast of success to the sports of the field. Then came the long road home. Raits was not reached until past eleven o'clock where, after supper and weak, warm lime punch all went cheerfully to bed.

As the autumn days shortened, Thornton grew anxious to return to Thornville to be in time for the fox-hunting season. But he was sorry to leave the north, for in point of country, weather, game and sport of every kind his most sanguine expectations were exceeded.

* So named because it was originally made for porters and other labourers. It was a dark brown, bitter beer, brewed from malt partly charred or browned by drying at a high temperature.

7 Old Balmoral Castle. This is the house which John Smith remodelled during the 1830s and which remained in use by the royal family while new Balmoral Castle was being built during 1853–6. A small memorial near the drive marks the site of the former building

CHAPTER 2

A Sporting Resort

It was a happy hour when the Sassenach discovered
the pleasure to be gained from renting a Northern grouse moor.
The Revd H. A. Macpherson, 1895

If Colonel Thornton's sporting expeditions were unique, he himself was un-representative of aristocratic attitudes towards shooting in the 18th century. Gentlemen looked down on field sports, occupying themselves with the politer accomplishments of dancing, fencing and elegant horsemanship. Lord Chesterfield wrote to his godson, 'Eat as much game as you please, but I hope you will never kill any yourself; and, indeed, I think you are above any of these rustick, illiberal sports of guns, dogs, horses, which characterise our English Bumpkin Country Gentlemen.' That bumpkin had been satirised by Addison in the early part of the century in his portrait of the old English sportsman whose walls were covered with the horns of deer he had killed in the chase and which he thought the most valuable furniture of his house.

Left to himself, Charles Savile glanced curiously round the room. There were the Colonel's three Purdeys and a couple of rook-rifles gleaming in a tall mahogany case beside the washstand. Two leather gun-cases and two vast cartridge magazines, worn with travel and covered with innumerable labels, were in a corner, alongside the Colonel's capacious leather shooting-seat with its aluminium fittings. On a great rack shone, tier by tier, his seventeen pairs of boots and shoes, the lowest row dedicated to well-greased ankle-boots with their anklets around them. There was something marvellously polished and perdurable about this congregation of footwear, on which it seemed time could lay no decaying finger.

The bookcase did not hold many books: the Badminton Library, *Autumns in Aberdeenshire*, *Thirty Years of Sport in Central India*, *High Pheasants in Theory and Practice*, *The Keeper's Book*, a manual of game-rearing, *The Improvement of Partridge Manors*, and *The Diary of Colonel Peter Hawker*. Beside them were the twenty stout volumes of the Colonel's own shooting-journal, in red leather stamped with his full name in gold. The pictures on the wall were all by Lodge or Thorburn, and most of them depicted partridges bursting over a high thorn fence in the instant before their dissolution, or grouse and pheasants as seen by the eye of their slayer in that perilous instant when they were about to cross the line of guns. (J. K. Stanford, *The Twelfth*, p. 30.)

The popularity of shooting had long been inhibited by the lack of a suitable weapon to use on winged game. 'If I miss sitting, I commonly hit 'em flying,' said Bellair in Mrs Centlivre's *Love at a Venture*, implying that it was only when the former failed that he tried the latter way. In fact it was often a combined operation; one man fired at the birds sitting and the other fired 'as soon as ever he . . . has pulled his tricker and flashes in the pan, or at least if you are very near as soon as you hear the report of his piece'. The awkwardness of the whole operation may be summed up in a quotation from J. Sprint, who, in a little book entitled *The Experienc'd Fowler*, published in 1700, declared that 'six foot is a sufficient length for the barrel of any piece, all above are unmanageable and tiresome.' A century later the Revd. W. B. Daniel said that within sixty years of when he wrote an individual who exercised the art of shooting birds on the wing was considered as performing something extraordinary. Crowds of curious people sought to attend the gunner so that they could be eyewitnesses of his feat.

By coincidence a contemporary of Daniel's, T. B. Johnson, wrote a delightful account of his first experience of grouse-shooting at Bowes. He took up quarters at a local inn on 11 August, and from the parlour window watched darkness fall

with much more than ordinary interest. On retiring to rest, the thought of the morrow continued so busy in my brain as to force me to reject the balmy embrace of the drowsy god for a very considerable length of time; and when at length a semi-repose came over me, my thoughts, no longer under the influence of reason, still wandered amongst the alpine regions I was about to ascend. Long before the day dawned, I was roused from my reverie by my guide (a person well acquainted with the mountains is an indispensable auxiliary) who appeared as anxious for the expected sport as myself. After a dejeune or repast, hastily swallowed, we sallied forth; but when we reached the edge of the moor, the faint grey streaks of the eastern horizon afforded not half-light sufficient to discern the flight of a bird. We paused. The scene, though enveloped in dense darkness, was highly interesting; I could perceive the lofty mountains frowning through the deep gloom, while the dogs whined impatiently by my side, and

8 *A brace of setters, steady at point, and down charge! The lengthy process of reloading (centre) enabled dogs to recover their wind*

the moor-cock uttered his early call, thus announcing the near approach of morning. At length day might be said to dawn; when through the heavy grey which still hung upon the hills, I saw the flash of a gun, and by the time the whizzing sound reached my ears, another flash blazed near the same spot; a proof that there were others more impatient than myself.

I placed my foot for the first time upon the grouse mountains, and my shoe was instantly filled with water, from the pearly drops with which the heather was heavily laden: those who pursue the moor-cock must make up their mind to walk with wet feet. The dogs worked hard for nearly half an hour before they were able to recognise the proximity, or indeed the traces, of game: an old cock rose—I heard him chatter, but could not distinctly see him, and therefore did not fire. After some time, I was delighted to observe the dogs draw in a manner which left no doubt of game being before them. They stood; I went up to them, and paused in anxious suspense. They moved on: the birds were evidently running before them; and it was not till after some lapse of time, and the birds had run a quarter of mile that I heard the old cock give the signal for his family to rise; three of the brood rose quite within distance, yet they appeared so nearly the colour of the heath over which they flew, that my aim was confused, and I missed them. I could not mark them down, but my guide said he saw 'them drop to an inch'. I could scarcely believe him; however, he had been used to the business, and smiled at my incredulity. He led me to the very spot. The dogs drew and immediately came to that sort of point which indicated that the game was under their noses. 'Don't be in a hurry, Sir,' said my guide. I took his advice, and picked doublets! I was delighted. I swallowed a sandwich and washed it down with all possible gusto.

By happy chance the end of the Napoleonic Wars coincided with radical improvements to firearms which culminated in the celebrated gunsmith Joseph Manton producing flintlocks of the same size and dimension as guns today. Since the 1760s when the customary fowling piece had a barrel about 42 in. long and a wood stock to the muzzle, a stream of developments had taken place. Demand for a lighter weapon led first to the barrel being reduced to about 36 in. and later to the wood stock being reduced to the conventional fore-end. The over-and-under revolving barrel action was replaced by the side-by-side double barrel with ribbing and finally, in the hands of Manton, the short, squat stock was altered to the drop and curve used ever since.

If, however, the sportsman had to wait sixty years from the Manton era to the era of smokeless powder, by the early 1800s there were improvements parallel to guns in the shape of Dollond's new telescope and the express rifle. The latter replaced a weapon whose bullet formed a trajectory similar to an arrow shot from a bow. The work of a man who wanted to shoot grouse and the work of the man who wanted to stalk deer were made practical at last.

That Scotland became a popular sporting resort early in the 19th century was due not only to its place in the Romantic Movement and hence its powerful allure for tourists, but also because of the condition of agriculture in England. This was the period of land enclosure, brought about by the high price of corn in the wars. Wheat rose from 43s a quarter in 1792 to over £6 in 1812, which encouraged the bringing of waste lands into production and the enclosing of the old commons and open field systems. As high grain prices stimulated output rents rose and landlords had more cash to make new enclosures. Farming became a good investment; the yield on traditional investment, namely government stocks, in no way compared with the yield from grain crops, and in any case war is never conducive to the stability of capital values of fixed interest securities.

Far-reaching consequences for the shooting man took place. Long stubbles disappeared as the threshing machine, introduced to the north of England in the 1790s, spread southwards. The rough land—ideal for birds to lie close in for

9 The First Barrel *by Abraham Cooper, R.A. (1787–1868)*

pointers and setters—was greatly reduced, while the numbers of people taking up shooting as a sport increased. Even woodland cover was getting sparse; felling had been encouraged by a succession of bad harvests in the latter part of the 18th century, when landlords had recourse to timber to meet their debts. Latterly, there had been heavy demand for timber for naval ships, the burning of charcoal and the construction of post and rail fences for enclosures.

It is true that many of these changes were taking place only gradually and in

10 *Victorious Victorians in the north of England*

their initial stages were beneficial to shooting men. The swede turnip, for example, was a grand cover crop when broadcast, but when the drill was introduced birds took to running along the rows out of range of the gunner. The man who farmed his own land could farm as he wished; it was the creation of game 'preserves' which restricted the amount of sport available to a privileged few and, incidentally, created considerable revulsion against shooting.

It was partly due to better communications, roads to start with and later railways, which led to the country house party becoming part of the social round. Guests had to be entertained, the battue was an easy answer and rural relaxation came to be identified with field sports. In later years Augustus Hare was to comment that 'it can hardly appear an unmixed good that the owners of these historic mansions only last in them during the shooting and hunting seasons. But probably this state of things will continue as long as the silly mania for what is called sport prevails, and while the youth of the richer classes—upper I will not call them, are in general brought up more like young gamekeepers than anything else.'[1]

If the exclusive world of those shooting men who guarded their game preserves with jealous care contrasted ill with the democracy of hunting, there were plenty of sportsmen who preferred or sought the old, simple ways and turned to the unspoiled hills of Scotland or northern England for their sport. Technology in its various forms pointed the way for them: the shotgun was now easy to handle, agricultural inventions had not touched the hills, those hills were easier of access, and the rivers were relatively unpolluted by effluent. This last factor was relevant, for most shooting men like to vary their recreation with a little fishing and many of the English rivers were becoming unfishable. The last salmon caught in the Thames, for example, was in 1821.

Meanwhile in Scotland indigenous shooting parties were becoming an established feature of the autumn scene, paving the way for the English invasion. Country innkeepers spoke of the trade they gained through sport and itinerant workers, such as the men employed by farmers to kill vermin, took on the role of gillie. Mrs Grant of Rothiemurchus described the social setting in Inverness-shire in 1815, which was no doubt enacted similarly elsewhere. Country houses, inns and farmhouses were packed with people making merry with fishing and shooting, rides and walks, dinners and dances, picnics to distant lochs and glens. The Pitmain Tryst and the Inverness Meeting were already annual highlights of the season.

All this reflected the fact that autumn in the country is a traditional time for relaxation before the winter, a time when, for our forebears, gaiety was combined with the serious business of gathering and preparing the fruits of the earth for the lean season. Oatmeal was ground, herring salted, vegetables dried, fruit preserved, sheep and deer tongues smoked. Shooting was only one facet of the work involved, and because it was work the lairds shot little themselves, employing their gamekeepers as game killers to provide their masters' households with meat. The light weapons of the early 19th century enabled the masters to go out and enjoy doing their own killing.

From such humble beginnings derived a sport which was to become world renowned, and by 1820 to shoot grouse was to be a fashionable Englishman. The moor was a refuge from London life, and when the prosecution of Queen Caroline compelled the House of Lords to sit through the stifling heat of August adjourning only between 9 September and 3 October, Lord Holland commented that,

> In this terrible matter which brings us to town
> We shall all be knocked up if we are not knocked down.
> None surely will gain by this 'Call of the House',
> Save eldest sons, witnesses, lawyers and grouse.[2]

So popular did shooting become that the novelist Emily Eden wrote in 1826 that in the shooting season men would travel only on Sundays.[3] She lamented the fact that her brother, as Auditor of the Accounts of Greenwich Hospital, had to investigate a case of embezzlement there and was thus deprived of his August holiday on the moors. But matters could be taken too far, and she was properly critical of the suitor who failed to propose to a lady. 'Probably,' she remarked, 'in the way men usually do he settled that though he could propose any day, he could go out grouse-shooting only on the Twelfth, and while the grouse might grow wild she would remain tame, so that he had better attend to the grouse first and woo the lady later.'[4]

Joseph Manton's success in perfecting a flintlock that was sufficiently light did not coincide with all and sundry being able to use it. Not until 1831 did the Whig legislation repeal the burdensome game laws which made it illegal for anyone to buy or sell game and illegal for anyone who was not a squire or a squire's eldest son to kill game. About the time of repeal the letting of sporting rights began to be an accepted practice in Scotland. Until then landlords waxed fat on high rents paid to them by Lowland farmers. The tragedy of the Clearances, with its rights and wrongs, is another matter, but the prosperity which the sheep flocks had brought the landed classes was dwindling rapidly. Although to some extent Highland landowners considered it beneath their dignity to let sporting rights, the shortage of sport was due not so much to conscious reluctance on the part of the lairds to let their land as to the idea of anyone but the laird living on and enjoying the perquisites of an estate being so alien as to be incomprehensible.

If a Highland proprietor was disposed to sell an estate early in the century there was not much inducement to even a keen sportsman to buy; land did not rank as a possible speculation and with communications primitive it was better to rent each year if one could and leave the options open. In many cases landlords could not sell anyway; the 'yird hunger', the passion for possessing land, was strong in the Scot and it was thought that to abolish entail would be to make it possible that a lord should be a landless beggar, which would be an unspeakable degradation to the great order of nobility. Not until 1848 was an Act passed for regulating and for abolishing entails under certain conditions. Within a generation two-thirds of Highland estates changed hands.

With the way now open for the English to purchase Highland properties, royal precept and example gave impetus to the trend. Significantly in the same year as the Entail Act was passed, Queen Victoria leased Balmoral from Lord Mar. Her first visit to Scotland had been in August 1842. On her tour she was entertained lavishly by Lord Breadalbane at Taymouth Castle; the whole setting seemed, she

11 *A Highland morning: Queen Victoria, Prince Albert and the royal family ascending Lochnagar, a few miles from Balmoral; engraving from a painting by Carl Haag*

said, as if some great chieftain of feudal times was receiving his sovereign, and the desire to have a home in the Highlands was implanted in her. Bonfires were lit on the hilltops, reels were danced by torchlight in front of the house and Prince Albert, attended by 300 Highlanders, went shooting.

Balmoral was not the first property the Queen looked at. In 1847, on the yacht *Victoria and Albert*, she did a reconnaissance. From the start the trip was inauspicious; fog forced them to run into Dartmouth the day after leaving Osborne, the rain poured down, the royal yacht rolled and the Queen was ill in consequence. Eventually she landed at Fort William and drove to Ardverikie, then the property of Lord Abercorn, on the shore of Loch Laggan. Alas, the rain had dampened even her enthusiasm. There was, she remarked in her Journal, little to say of her stay; the country was very fine, but the weather was most dreadful.

The discovery of Balmoral the following year was due to the son of the royal physician, Sir James Clark, who had gone to stay there with the then lessee, Sir Robert Gordon, and sent a glowing report of the place. The death of Gordon made it available, and both the Queen and Prince Albert fell in love with it at first sight. 'It was so calm, and so solitary, it did one good as one gazed around; and the pure mountain air was most refreshing. All seemed to breathe freedom and peace, and to make one forget the world and its sad turmoils.'

Of the pleasures of the Scottish countryside the Queen was no mere onlooker. She rejoiced in the hills, and the long journeys, taking delight in trying to retain her anonymity when she stayed at some village inn *en route* with her entourage. On their expeditions within the Estate the Queen would ride up the hills on her pony while Prince Albert shot grouse or ptarmigan or stalked deer and the children gathered Cairngorm stones. Her Journal reflected her liking for the qualities of the Highlanders, which in themselves have always been a potent factor in drawing the English to Scotland for sport. 'It's very pleasant', she recorded John Brown saying to her one day, 'to walk with a person who is always content.' And content she was, not least because such a blunt mode of address, lacking in obsequiousness, was a refreshing change from the manners of court life.

The happiness of family holidays at Balmoral led, in 1852, to the opportunity being taken of buying the estate with 17,400 acres for the sum of £31,500. A larger house than the existing one was needed, and the foundation stone was laid in 1853. Furnished with the Balmoral tartan of black, red and lavender on a grey background, designed by the Prince, with the Queen's own Victorian tartan and with the Royal and Hunting Stuart tartans, the best-known example of Scots Baronial was built. The seal was finally set on the popularity and fashion of the Scottish holiday, with all its concomitant sports and pastimes.

12 *Albert Edward, Prince of Wales, in 1865*

Delights Expected

CHAPTER 3
Taking A Moor

The North Mail

However flattering and plausible the advertisement of printed conditions may appear, it is of vital importance that a personal inspection of the ground . . . be made before the rent or conditions of let are seriously entertained. *Thomas Speedy, 1884*

In order to understand how grouse moors in Scotland became available to sportsmen it is necessary to outline the effect of man on the Highland landscape, and to trace the social and economic factors which caused hill land to be divided in its usage between grouse, sheep and deer.

Red grouse would not have become so numerous in Scotland had there not been wide expanses of moorland to sustain them, and the fact that such moorlands exist is due to the predatory nature of man. From the 9th century A.D. the Caledonian Forest of Scots pine and the scrub woodlands of ash, oak, alder and birch were cut or burned, for the building of boats, for use as domestic heating fuel or simply to flush out enemies from their hiding-places. Destruction continued through the centuries; Bruce burned the forests of Inverary in an expedition against Comyn, General Monk cut the wood round Aberfoyle to expose the hideouts of Royalist supporters in the Civil War. In the 18th century ironsmelting provided a new incentive; the forests of Strathspey, Glenmore and Rothiemurchus fed the hungry furnaces of the Industrial Revolution, and when the last of the forests was felled for ironworking early in the 19th century the demand of sheepmasters for grazing land gave fresh impetus to clearance.

After the Forty-five Rebellion a pleasure-seeking landed class in Scotland, weakened in its role of clan leadership, found solace in the social life of London. To sustain themselves in this relative luxury there came to these gentry at the end of the 18th century the welcome bonus of fat rents from southern sheep flocks. While the sheep destroyed scrub woodland by grazing, their masters wrought similar destruction by fire. Meanwhile other industries such as tanning and bobbin-making demanded birch, and as woodland retreated and heather took its place the landscape assumed its present form.

Demand for Highland sport would never have developed to the extent it did had it not been for an Act of Parliament in 1831 which widened the limited circle that had hitherto monopolised it. This Act provided that the former necessary qualifications as to birth and estate should no longer be indispensable to the killing of game within forest bounds, whenceforth 'any certificated person could do so, either on his own land or on the land of any other person with his permission'. Moreover, the sale of game was legalised, and the statute at the same time enacted more summary measures than those previously in force for protection against trespass. Enthusiasts of sport included all sorts and conditions of men. Scotsmen themselves took a prominent part, and the middle classes from both England and Scotland supplied the wealth to compete successfully in securing some of the best forests and moors. To own stalking in particular was to own the greatest of status symbols, and Lord George Scott remarked that the stalker would assume the same air of tolerant superiority over the shooter of grouse as an itinerant fox-hunter, whose two horses have been stabled for a season at Melton, may show towards a squire hunting in the provinces. Contemporaries held that to go out with a couple of setters and a fowling-piece when the red deer were roaring in the neighbourhood bordered on the contemptible, and that shooting grouse after red deer was like writing a sentiment in a lady's album after giving the finishing touch to a tragedy or an epic poem. Professor Blaikie expressed the viewpoint in a couplet which contains only that measure of deviation from the truth that is necessary to sustain an epigram:

> London brewers shoot the grouse,
> And lordlings shoot the deer.

Anthony Trollope, in satirical vein, described a similar situation in *The Duke's Children*. Crummie-Toddie

comprised an enormous acreage of so-called forest and moor. Mr Dobbes declared that nothing like it had as yet been produced in Scotland. Everything had been made to give way to deer and grouse. The thing had been managed so well that the tourist nuisance had been considerably abated. There was hardly a potato patch left in the district, not a head of cattle to be seen. There were no inhabitants remaining, or so few that they could be absorbed in game-preserving or cognate duties. Reginald Dobbes, who was very great at grouse, and supposed to be capable of outwitting a deer by venatial wiles more perfectly than any other sportsman in Great Britain regarded Crummie-Toddie as the nearest thing there was to a paradise on earth. Could he have been allowed to pass one or two special laws for his own protection, there might still have been improvement. He would have had a clause in his lease against the making of any new roads, opening of footpaths, or building of bridges. He had seen somewhere in print a plan for running a railway from Callander to Fort Augustus right through Crummie-Toddie! If this were done in his time the beauty of the world would be over.[1]

The growth of organised shooting in Scotland is reflected in the fact that game books first made their appearance towards the end of the 18th century. The upward trend in the number of licensed gamekeepers in Scotland is also interesting. There were 608 keepers in Scotland in 1836, 774 in 1853, 1,050 in 1868. The fact, however, that grouse shooting did not reach its zenith until the '80s and '90s can be explained partially in economic terms. The late 1820s and the 1830s formed a period of social unrest, with the landed interest feeling and being threatened by radicals. Confidence had returned by the '50s, when Britain was by far the richest country in the world, but social acceptance of those aristocrats of industry and commerce who formed such a large proportion of tenants or owners of grouse moors and deer forests towards the end of the century came only slowly. A powerful catalyst in the blurring of the title of gentleman was the public school, and as the territorial foundations of the aristocratic way of life began to be disregarded, a new aristocracy of business and professional talents emerged eager to savour country life and leisure.

Paradoxically the period of highest demand for sporting properties in Scotland occurred when fear of taxation was growing and land was mistrusted as a form of investment. The reason for this was that sporting in Scotland could be leased and a lease could be relinquished. Add to this the ease of travel and the fashion for long holidays in the autumn and the annual bandwagon to the north was to become an established custom.

Half a century or so earlier, in the 1820s and 1830s, the discerning sportsman could pick up shooting rights for practically nothing. An example of the rising trend in rents is Faskally, where two moors let on the estate for £8 in the 1830s commanded £800 in the 1880s. Lord Malmesbury recorded in his memoirs, published in 1884, that in 1833 he was offered the sporting rights of the island of Harris, including grouse moor, stalking and fishing for £25. Later in the century the island changed hands and the sporting rights were let for £2,000. The rise in freehold sporting values corresponded. About 1835 Joseph Mitchell was recommended to buy Glen Roy for £12,000 or £13,000. He declined, and it was bought by Mr Baillie of Bristol for £26,000 who sold it forty years later for £58,000.

Whether the sportsman had a full purse or a relatively empty one in early years, he had to have luck or good judgement to get fair sport. Published information was extremely scanty, and for those without social contacts in the north, the selection of a moor could only be done satisfactorily by going north oneself and making one's own investigations. Few shootings were advertised in *The Field* until late on in the century, sporting agents were unknown in London, and only Hugh Snowie, the Inverness gunmaker and sporting agent, was sufficiently enterprising to come down for ten days during the London season and interview prospective clients at the emporium of a Bond Street firm of opticians. The disaster that could befall a sportsman who rented a moor without adequate inquiry was exemplified by Patrick Chalmers's story of the Sassenach

who took a shoot in the Highlands without previous inspection of it even by proxy. When he would go into residence there, he drove upon a public coach for there was no railway. He was fortunate in getting a seat next to the driver, and, without disclosing himself, he sought local information about his bargain. He asked the coachman then, 'Do you know Auchenflichity?' 'Aye,' was the uncompromising answer. 'And what sort of place is Auchenflichity?' 'Gin the deil was tethered on it ye'd just say "puir brute".'[2]

Accessibility was another problem for seekers of moors. Those that were far from a railway were impracticable, while others within reach of a railway suffered depredations from poachers eager to supply the London market with grouse in time for the Twelfth. In the middle years of the century the indifference of landowners, eager for a peaceful life, was not conducive to discouragement of poaching. By stringent agreements with sheep tenants or crofters they could have prevented trespass on the hills more easily than tenants of shootings were able to, and bearing in mind the profit they made from sport it was both in their interest and their duty to preserve game. Yet every lessee of grouse-shooting was aware of how very little assistance and encouragement he got from nine proprietors out of ten.

Before setting out for the north the prudent novice would have consulted books such as Thomas Oakleigh's *Shooting Code* (1836). Oakleigh's catalogue of the grouse shooter's necessities ran as follows:

Dogs; fowling piece, in case or bag; two extra pivots; a pivot pricker; pivot-wrench, gun-rod, or cleaner; a small bottle of olive oil; some linen-cloth and leather; powder flask; dram-flask; shot belt; bird-bag; a canister of powder; a quantity of shot, various sizes; a few pairs of woollen stockings; strong laced boots; or strong shoes and gaiters; dark shooting dress; copper-caps and box; wadding; screw turner; spring cramp; a punch for cutting waddings; shoe oil; straps; collars, couples, and cords for leading and tying up dogs; dog-whistle; dog-whip; a pocket-knife, with an instrument attached for unlacing boots; a pen-knife; a pocket comb; some cord or string for tying up game; hampers, in which grouse may be packed between layers of heath; sealing-wax, and seal to mark birds when sent by coach or carrier; game certificate; card of permission, or other authority to produce to the game-keepers; sandwiches; cigars; soda-powders; Prometheans*; brandy.

Particular caution would have had to be exercised in the purchase of a gun. The market was full of spurious articles with forged names on locks and barrels or with forged proof marks. A change of spelling or initials was often made by the forger, who somehow thought that his crime was thus lessened. 'Greener' would be spelt 'Greenen', 'Purdey' became 'Purdy', and 'W. W. Greener' was christened with Horace or Albert. The wise thing to do before buying was to take the gun or rifle to the alleged maker to ascertain whether it was genuine or not.

If the budding sportsman, having read Oakleigh, sought other books on the circumstances of grouse-shooting, he would have found, at least until the late part of the century, the available literature rather daunting. Other sports were delineated as mere child's play compared to grouse-shooting and deer-stalking, and no recreation required greater personal exertion. Admonitions on physical training long before the beginning of the season began were apt and sensible and might be heeded more nowadays, but forebodings on the fate of the unfit tended to be rather gloomy. A good tip was to see that one was provided with a horse or a conveyance to ride or drive from the shooting ground, for that journey in itself could be over no mean distance. Shooters who boasted of their acquaintance with London gunmakers, and who told of their feats in the shooting galleries, and of having slain pigeons from traps at the celebrated Red House at Battersea, or pheasants in Lord Battue's preserves, were often woefully disappointed on their arrival in the north.

On the hill itself, all manner of reasons for disappointment were cited by writers. You were out of training and could not walk. Your equipment was incomplete. Your dogs, never having seen any winged game other than partridges and pheasants, would not point grouse. You got lost in the mist, for want of a

* Ancestors of the modern match, they consisted of a small glass tube, containing sulphuric acid, surrounded by an inflammable mixture, which ignited on being pressed.

14 *Room for reflection and relaxation far from London: the panelled opulence of Mar Lodge in Aberdeenshire*

guide, a pocket compass, or a previous intimate knowledge of the locality, and inadvertently became a trespasser, when a glorious row ensued, ending perhaps in a struggle for the encroacher's fowling piece. If not tired out by walking beyond your strength, probably over useless tracts, in the early morning, that object would be most effectively accomplished in the hot sun at noon, and you would be rendered not only incapable of following up the sport in the afternoon but on the following morning also. As for quarters, some tavern would have to suffice, if such a house could call itself a tavern where oatcake and peat supplied the place of bread and fuel.

If the wherewithal for physical self-indulgence was at hand, it had to be guarded against. Total abstinence from alcohol was advised, though a little well-diluted cognac was permissible. Wine was frowned upon as making people more thirsty. The handbook of the deer-stalker was perhaps preferable to many other guides, for while William Scrope advised his stalker to go abstemiously to the hill he conceded that to restrict him from the venison pasty would be cruel. He was allowed tea and a few grapes to cool himself, and peaches and nectarines might be put in his pocket, for 'as he was sure to sit upon them they would do no earthly harm but rather confer a benefit by moistening the outward man'.

The importance of suitable clothing to preserve the health of the sportsman was properly stressed. As, it was explained, grouse frequented bleak and exposed moors, mists and storms had constantly to be guarded against. The ideal material of dress was therefore woollen. On hot days the hardy might have ventured to put on a linen jacket, but those who were subject to rheumatism or colds were cautioned against the chill so often felt on reaching the mountaintop. Flannel waistcoats and drawers, therefore, were strongly advised and, above all, worsted stockings. Waterproof footwear was important and boots were better than shoes. The latter collected the tops of heather inside them which rubbed off the skin. A little candle-grease rubbed over the feet prevented them being stripped.

The tourist and sporting attractions of Scotland led to an awareness on the part of Scottish servants that here lay a new source of revenue. Thornton had com-

15 *Ideal protection for sufferers from rheumatism when venturing on bleak, misty moors. An advertisement from* Something About Guns and Shooting (*1891 edn.*) *by 'Purple Heather'*

plained of being constantly overcharged for services rendered, and recommended other gentlemen '. . . to make a previous agreement with every countryman whose services they may want, but in particular with a Highlander: many of them have but one idea, which is, that an Englishman is a walking mint . . .'. A little good-natured bargaining was probably sufficient to induce the correct terms. In 1860 Charles Weld met with a demand from his gillies for 3s a day besides breakfast, lunch and an unlimited quantity of whisky provided. Taking counsel together, Weld and his friends decided that as sturdy women worked in the fields for 10d a day, and two of them would be more than equal to one gillie, it would create a sensation to go on the moors attended by twelve muscular damsels. With assumed gravity the sportsmen told their male attendants of their intentions, who swiftly modified their terms of service.

To be fair to those who traded with English sportsmen the season was a short one, particularly before the building of modern shooting-lodges enabled visitors to relax on wet days in some comfort, and before the introduction of driving grouse lengthened the shooting season. The point was illustrated by Rab McKellar, landlord of the Argyll Hotel in Inverary who, when an Englishman protested at his bill, saying that he could live cheaper in the best hotel in London, replied, 'Oh, nae doot, Sir—Nae doot ava—but do you no' ken the reason?' 'No, not a bit of it,' said the stranger hastily. 'Weel then,' replied the host, 'as ye seem to be a gey sensible callant, I'll tell ye; there's 365 days in the Lunnon hotel-keeper's calendar, but we have only three months in ours!—Do ye understand me noo, frien'?—We maun make hay in the Hielans when the sun shines, for it's unco seldom she dis't!'[3]

Meanness on the part of the employer would sometimes rebound. Boaty, a fishing gillie thus named on the Dee, was attending an angler one day who caught salmon after salmon. Between each fish he consoled himself with a pull from his flask, which he returned to his pocket without offering a dram to Boaty. The latter, having reached the point of exasperation, pulled the boat ashore, shouldered the oars and all the fishing gear and set off homewards. His master, far from considering his day's work to be over, peremptorily ordered him to come back. 'Na, na,' replied the offended Boaty, 'them 'at drink by themsells may just fish by themsells.'

If, undeterred by what he had learnt from the north, a sportsman decided to take a lease of a moor, he might have expected to have a wider choice as time went on. Hugh Snowie's first list of shootings to let was printed in 1836 and it contained only eight advertisements. By 1872 he sent out three or four lists every year and circulated them to the extent of 1,500 copies. In the latter year he said that demand for shootings in the north was so great that he was able to let everything on his list and rents were getting higher and higher every year. Also, moors and deer forests were being taken so much on long leases that in future there would be fewer on the market.

In 1865 the author W. A. Adams carefully watched the advertisements in *The Field* and other papers, and in the spring he noted the following advertisement one Saturday:

> To be let, the shootings of Glenmarkie, in Aberdeenshire and Banffshire, extending over 11,000 acres of moor and low ground; references to last tenant. Application to be made to Mr Snowie, of Inverness, or the Law Agents in Edinburgh.

Adams wrote the same evening to the Law Agents, asking them to call first thing on Monday morning upon the advertisers (thus the speed of the post) and telegraph him the rent and the name of the last tenant. The reply was prompt, the rent £265, and the former tenant reported the moor to be excellent.

By 10 a.m. on the Tuesday Adams had taken a seven-year lease at £265, having telegraphed his Edinburgh agents, and his swift action was justified by the fact that a Staffordshire gentleman had written to accept on the Tuesday instead of sending a telegram and had thus found the matter concluded.

Adams visited the moor and remedied the fact that it was insufficiently burnt. Three weeks' shooting subsequently produced 370 brace over dogs, shooting four days a week, with only two guns.

The following year, 1866, was equally successful, but disease struck at the end of the season and not until 1870 was the stock adequate for culling once more. By that time the lease was within two years of expiry, and although Adams was anxious to renew, his partner was not. In the event the decision was right, though for unexpected reasons. The proprietor, anticipating the Ground Game Act of 1880 by a few years, whereby occupiers of land became entitled to kill ground game for protection of their husbandry, suddenly informed his crofter tenants that they could kill ground game on their arable land. Adams foresaw a deterioration of his low ground sport and departed.

His next venture came about through his meeting William Dunbar, a visionary who foresaw the future importance of sport in the Highlands. Dunbar not only made his living by taking shootings and fishings from Caithness proprietors, he also urged upon them the need to build roads and lodges, keepers' houses and kennels. The proprietors knew little about how to introduce sporting subjects to southern sportsmen, and in Dunbar they found a skilled and honest agent.

Adams negotiated the lease of 24,000 acres of Dulnawillan, Chullacan and Backlas, at the rent of £560, proprietor paying all rates and taxes, and tenant paying the keeper and all other expenses. The lease was for seventeen years, and Adams's friends told him he was crazy to tie himself up for such a term of years. In the course of his lease sport had its ups and downs, but he was correct in assuming that as railways crept up rents would rise. Tenants who acted likewise were often able to sub-let half their moors and get their own shooting free.

By the 1890s, however, long leases had become unusual. The choice of sporting places had become much wider, and tenants were keener to change the scene of their sport from time to time. More places on the sporting lists each year in turn increased the agents' knowledge, and their approach became more professional. Annual visits of inspection were made to moors, game book records tabulated, and photographs of lodges procured. The normal agent's commission was 5 per cent charged on the rental paid by the proprietor and shooting tenant in equal proportions. The important thing was that there was now a choice of agents from whom to seek information, and competition had forced them to provide a good service.

In that respect, a most valuable publication appeared for the first time in 1873 entitled *The Sportsman's Guide*. Edited by J. Watson-Lyall, at that time editor of a provincial newspaper in Perth, it appeared twice a year for over thirty years and was so successful that the business was moved to London. The guide contained the names and addresses of every moor worthy of the name, as well as other shootings and fishings in Scotland. Another firm which migrated from Perth to London was Paton's. Originally gunmakers, a sporting agency was opened in Mount Street in the 1870s. The business prospered, the gunmaking side was abandoned, and while the elder Paton ran the London office his son personally inspected every moor or forest placed in their hands for letting.

A comfortable holiday on the grouse moor could, however, be obtained at no cost. Evan MacKenzie estimated in 1895 that 5,000 out of 6,000 sportsmen who travelled northwards annually incurred no outlay beyond their rail fare. These lucky fellows comprised several categories, the first of which was described by MacKenzie as the jolly party assembled by Mr Shorters-Court, the well-known stockbroker. Half a dozen of his best clients could rely every autumn on their broker's invitation to shoot his grouse and drink his champagne upon the heather. They accepted his hospitality yearly as discount on the gross amount of the annual commissions they paid him, and their host regarded his moor purely as a business speculation, a factor in the making of his pile, and the expense as all incurred in the way of business. So he treated his clients royally and, if they were enabled to enjoy good grouse-shooting for nothing, their business orders during the remainder of the year amounted to a sum that made Mr Shorters-Court's annual outlay in the Highlands appear a very insignificant item in his accounts.

On a neighbouring moor the Smythe-Brownes would be entertaining a large and fashionable party, principally bachelors, for the Misses Smythe-Browne were a host in themselves. They were the four somewhat plain-looking daughters of old Mr James Smyth Brown, who had added the hyphen and the final 'e's when he retired from business with a fortune. His daughters would scarcely feel so happy as they appeared to be if they quite realised that a free sojourn during the autumn on a crack grouse moor was the moving cause of all the kind attention they received during the London season from the half-dozen exquisites who were now slaughtering their father's grouse. Mr Smythe-Browne himself was shrewd enough to see through the game, but his inmost feelings were subdued by the desire of his family to take the position in society which they considered their wealth entitled them to hold.

Not so pleasant was the *modus operandi* of the shady man-about-town who, with one or two accomplices, systematically conned some innocent fellow who joined their syndicate. The name of the victim was inserted in the lease, one who would find himself hard put to secure the others' share of expenses. On wet days, the billiard and card tables of the shooting-lodge were used to fleece him, and in fine weather bets on bag-making capabilities were laid, subsequent shooting prowess depending on which way those bets were laid.

More venial was the conduct of the impecunious old sportsmen who rented wild but extensive moors and took in guns, perfectly aware of the scarcity of game. Their shooting partners were taken on at a fixed charge, to cover every requisite for the season, which it was shrewdly insisted should be paid in advance. The grumbles of these fellows when they found out the deception was a light cross to bear for an old sportsman whose skin was as tough as his love of shooting was unquenchable.

16 '*I am Mr Simpson and party*': an
illustration engraved on wood from
E. Lennox Peel's A Highland
Gathering (*1885*)

The Olden Times *by Charles Cooper Henderson. One of the disagreeable features of travelling by stage-coach was the start long before dawn* (Fores Ltd, London)

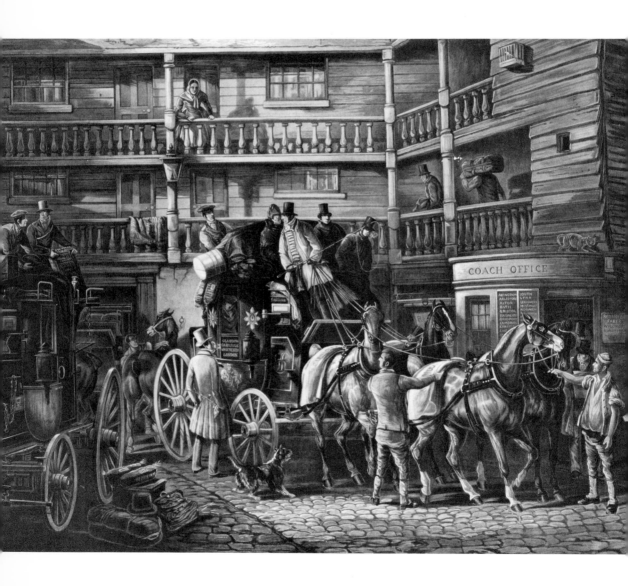

CHAPTER 4

The Journey North

Reader, whilst you whisk along in your cosy first-class carriage to Scotland, by the express on that best of all lines, the Great Northern, doing your forty miles, or even more, an hour, with your comfortable foot-warmer, *The Times* in your hand, and probably your pipe in your mouth, does it ever enter your head that the 400 miles that it takes you ten hours, or even less, to accomplish, were not performed under two days and two nights by your old father, or even in a longer time 'by poor dear old grandpapa', who considered that a railroad was an invention of the devil, and who declared that he would never do any thing but post if railways were permitted to travel at a greater rate than fifteen miles an hour? *C. T. S. Birch Reynardson, 1875*

'It is not easy for a modern Englishman, who can pass in a day from his club in St James's Street to his shooting-box among the Grampians, and who finds in his shooting-box all the comforts and luxuries of his club, to believe that, in the time of his great-grandfathers, St James's Street had as little connection with the Grampians as with the Andes.'

Macaulay wrote these words in his *History of England* in 1848. They show that the accessibility of Scotland to English sportsmen was as good then as it is now. Yet only sixty years before the publication of Macaulay's book, when Thornton made his grand tours, Scotland was virtually a closed book to sportsmen. Railways were to blaze the trail for the great age of grouse moor and deer forest, for the Twelfth to become a charmed number and Euston and King's Cross magic names.

In the 18th century the journey to Scotland was a hazardous undertaking, and the hazards were exaggerated through ignorance and prejudice. The geography of the country was not an asset in its favour. If he entered Scotland on the east the traveller would not have far to go before being pleasantly surprised by Edinburgh, but if he went by the dreary country of Dumfriesshire and the moors of Galloway, a bleak and barren landscape destitute of trees, he would soon have misgivings. Already, of course, he would have been warned by the Northumbrians, jealous of southern traders, that Scotland was the most barbarous country in the world, and the length, expense and discomfort of the journey he had so far endured would not have strengthened his morale.

Regular communications between London and Edinburgh dated from 1635, when a mail service by runners was made from the original Post Office in Eastcheap. The journey took three days, but the carrier was not habitually over-burdened for on one occasion as late as 1746 there was only one letter to deliver. The conveyance of passengers by coach began in 1658, when a stage-coach was tried, the price being £4 10s and the advertised time three weeks. It could not have had a great appeal, for even in 1754 a coach ran only once a month between the capitals. In that year the Edinburgh Stage-Coach, with steel springs and glass windows, was advertised to do the journey in ten days in summer, twelve in winter. Progress was made in 1788 when Palmer of the Bath theatre ran a service from London to Glasgow which took sixty-five hours. Comfort, however, did not increase in proportion to the speed of the journey; a stage-coach carried six passengers inside, and broke the stages in such an irregular way that food and sleep could be acquired only with difficulty. The increase in speed also meant an increase in accidents. In 1785 a correspondent to a newspaper begged coach proprietors to direct their servants, when a coach had been overturned, 'not to drag the passengers out at the window, but to replace the coach on its wheels first, provided it can be accomplished with the strength they have with them'.

Besides the danger and length of the journey to Scotland it was both tedious and expensive. Sir Richard Steele took with him a Frenchman to improve his knowledge of language, an expense that was partly mitigated by the travel allowance of £50 he received as one of the commissioners of inquiry into the forfeited estates. Scots Members of Parliament rode on horseback and often tried to reduce their costs by selling their horses at the other end. If even horseback was too expensive they could travel partly on pack-horses and partly on foot, as Tobias Smollett did in 1739.

Mail coaches, which were quicker and more punctual than stage, were introduced in 1784. They were also more comfortable—four passengers inside and three outside—and more expensive, the cost of the journey being about 15 guineas with tips and meals included. The most comfortable conveyance was the post-chaise, which carried only two passengers and enabled them to pick and choose the inns at which they fed and stayed.

The alternative to the road was the sea, on which plied packet ships which carried both goods and passengers. Uncertainty as to the duration and course of the journey was the distinction of this form of travel—witness Colonel Thornton's seaborne expedition. Steamer travel within Scotland was pioneered by Henry

18 Going to the Moors: *from a picture of the 1840s by Charles Cooper Henderson* (Fores Ltd, London)

Bell who, having established services on the Clyde and Forth, turned his attention further north. One steamer, the *Comet*, plied between Glasgow and Fort William, having previously gone between Glasgow and Greenock, while the *Stirling Castle*, whose route was between Leith and Stirling, Bell placed on the east of the Caledonian Canal between Inverness and Fort Augustus. This was prior to the complete opening of the canal in 1822; subsequently, both steamers ran between Inverness and Glasgow. Both Bell's vessels eventually came to grief and navigation of the canal was taken up by Messrs Burns, who in 1850 were running the vessels *Cygnet* and *Lapwing*. Later an official of the firm, David Hutcheson, took over the business and built up a fleet of vessels which embraced the west coast and Hebrides. Hutcheson died in 1881 and the business passed to his junior partner, MacBrayne.

Within the Highlands communications were appalling, and in 1724 General Wade emphasised the necessity for roads to be built to enable troops to operate more easily in the hills. Major improvements had to wait for Telford, but the 250 miles of road which Wade built were the earliest attempt at recognising the problems of the Highlands then and now as being those of communications. Even so, remote areas remained inaccessible for the practical purposes of sportsmen. The construction of minor roads in many parts of the Highlands stemmed from the time of the potato blight, 1846–8. With government aid, landed proprietors prevented men from starving by employing them on building roads, and the coastline from Loch Torridon to Loch Broom, for example, was linked by a highway which in due course became a county road.

By contrast, the principal routes to the Highlands were well used by tourists quite early in the century. Those who were not gregarious but whose journeys took them to the most popular places, such as the Trossachs, complained that the countryside swarmed with spruce cockneys in plaid waistcoats and so-called Glengarry bonnets, all of whom fancied themselves facsimiles of Roderick Dhu or James Fitz-James and quoted Sir Walter Scott to young ladies in tartan scarves. From the steamers that plied on the lochs came music and laughter and clouds of black smoke while coaches were festooned with bunches of heather in the same manner as car bonnets are adorned today.

To reach the Highlands from Edinburgh the traveller had the choice of several routes. The most obvious was the Highland road, by coach from Edinburgh to Perth and thence up through Dunkeld, Blair Atholl, Dalwhinnie and Carrbridge. If it was desired to travel all the way by steamer there was the direct journey up the east coast to Inverness, while for those in no hurry a steamer from Glasgow through the Caledonian Canal provided both the most comfortable and the most beautiful scenery. The captains of the boats were, it was said, 'well versed in the history of these localities, and also are most obliging and attentive to all strangers, in pointing out and explaining every thing that is worth seeing'.

North of Inverness, Tain or Invergordon could be reached by land or sea, and to reach Sutherland one could travel either by the mail-carriage, which in the 1840s was a kind of open phaeton which took several passengers and went twice a week northward and as often south, or by hiring a horse and suitable machine. The latter alternative gave one more independence and cost 4s or 5s a day, exclusive of the horse's keep.

One of the disagreeable features of travelling by stage-coach was the unholy hour of the morning start. It was quite customary to rise at 4 a.m. and Herbert Byng Hall[1] on a return journey from Inverness to Perth was compelled to leave at 2 a.m., 'of all hours probably the most inconvenient and most objectionable . . . should you retire early for a few hours rest previous to your departure, at the very moment that you sink into a sound nap, the horn of the guard apprises you of that, which the waiter, notwithstanding the strict injunctions he has received to arouse you in good time, of course has omitted; thus leaving you only a few minutes for slipping on your breeks and taking your seat; whereas, should you endeavour, by snoozing on a sofa, to prepare for your journey, you arise feverish and fatigued before that journey has actually commenced'.

In winter there was a choice of discomforts, with the interior being preferable perhaps to the rigours of outside travel, though, as Alexander Innes Shand[2] described it, 'even the originally agreeable pressure of the most fascinating of her sex might pall on you on the interminable stretch of highway between London and Newcastle. It was much more likely that luck would be against you, with a corpulent lady by your side and a portly gentleman opposite. Then difficulties would arise about dovetailing the legs, and any movement to get at the handkerchief or snuff-box would provoke scowling looks or shrill remonstrance. There might be the man with the hacking cough or the mother with the squalling baby. The nets above were bulging with umbrellas, hats and loose parcels, while the pockets were stuffed with bottles and packets of sandwiches.'

Accidents, though rare in terms of the volume of traffic, could be a nuisance. Lord Malmesbury[3] was travelling to Achnacarry when 'just after we had passed Gairlochy, we were stopped by my Keeper, who made us all get out (of the coach) as a bridge had fallen in: without him we should infallibly have gone over into a very deep burn. My servants, too, had a very dangerous journey by sea, their steamer having run aground between Aberdeen and Inverness; they saved their lives, but lost all their baggage and some of ours.'

Barring accidents, and given some discomfort, the sportsman could reach his grouse moor quite early in the 19th century by means of a sophisticated transport system on the main trunk routes. By 1820 thirty stage-coaches were leaving London for Edinburgh every day, thirteen to Glasgow, nine to Aberdeen, three to Inverness and three to Whitehaven. Split-second timing at each stage was a matter of pride, the team of four being changed in less than one minute. Speed was essential, bearing in mind the number of changes required. The London to Edinburgh Mail made twenty-eight changes, thus requiring 112 horses over the whole route. The coaching system in Britain was the envy of the world in its heyday, and in the 1830s the journey to Glasgow from London was taking only forty-two hours, a matter of twenty minutes quicker than the journey to Edinburgh.

Meanwhile the routes northward from the Lowlands of Scotland were being opened up with speed and enthusiasm. Whereas at the beginning of the century coaches were virtually unheard of north of Perth, by 1820 coach-routes threaded the glens, thanks to the rapidly developed network of roads and bridges engineered by Telford. By the mid-1830s the mail coach was leaving Edinburgh at four o'clock in the afternoon and arriving in Inverness by 10.30 the following morning. This conveyance was known as the 'God Permit', from its advertisement in the Caledonian Hotel, Inverness, '. . . to run South each Thursday, if God Permit'. The pioneer of the northern routes was an association of country gentlemen, notably Ramsay of Barnton, Barclay of Ury and Lord Glen Lyon, afterwards Duke of Atholl. They started a coach between Edinburgh and Aberdeen, and later another between Inverness and Aberdeen which was so efficient and successful that other coaches were encouraged to follow suit. Time was kept to the minute by the drivers and guards of the 'Defiance' coaches, resplendent in their uniforms of red coats and yellow collars, and even a vet was employed to see that the horses were properly cared for.

Yet with sad abruptness the coaching age drew to a close as the railways spread. Many mourned the change, regretting the loss of informality, simplicity and colourfulness which commercial awareness was bringing about. The laird, needful of money through sheer economic circumstance, through his custom of living it up in London or because of the fashion for sending his sons to an English public school, had let his sporting to the city merchant. To the latter's offices in Lombard Street came the telegram alerting him to the state of his moor or the coming condition of the river and he could jump into a hansom for the night train, to turn up the following morning on the platform at Perth or Inverness. The railways not only ran up the rents but wrought a revolution in the countryside. When remote glens could only be penetrated by coach or cart the sportsman was so rare that he was a welcome and an honoured guest with the Celtic innkeepers. The best parlour and bedroom were placed at his disposal, the fattest fowl was killed for him and a flask of the mellowest Glenlivet came forth from the recesses of the cellar. The railways so changed things that only by booking a week beforehand could room be guaranteed. Even then one of the parlours was made to do duty for a 'coffee-room', and the dinner table was hustled away in the corner. The house was crowded from ground floor to garret with Saxons from the Stock Exchange or Inns of Court who had run up for a ten-day holiday, and though they were capital fellows in ordinary circumstances the sentiments of jealous repulsion were mutual.

Romantic conservatives looked back on the coaching age with nostalgia, as many look back on the age of the steam locomotive today. The long, uncomfortable, expensive journey by road could not bear comparison with the ease of

THE HIGHLAND RAILWAY

(VIA PERTH AND DUNKELD.)

THE SHORTEST, QUICKEST AND MOST CONVENIENT ROUTE FOR FAMILIES AND SPORTSMEN, BETWEEN ENGLAND AND THE SOUTH OF SCOTLAND, AND : : : ALL PARTS OF THE HIGHLANDS. : : :

Through Carriages and Sleeping Saloons, London (Euston, King's Cross and St. Pancras) to Inverness, nightly, during the tourist season.

Enquiries respecting rates, fares, etc., should be addressed to MR. T. McEWEN, Traffic Manager, Inverness.

ROBERT PARK,

Inverness.   General Manager.

railway travel, and within a very few years the train journey to Scotland for the autumn holiday was to generate its own popular literature. But at least in one respect one can sympathise with the mourners of the coaches' demise, in their objection that an essential element of the joy of swift movement, namely the *sense* of speed was eliminated. The boast of more velocity, wrote De Quincey, rested upon alien evidence; because it was *said* that a train was travelling at sixty miles an hour it did not mean that it was being felt as a personal experience. Seated on a mail coach no evidence was needed to indicate the velocity achieved—it was seen and felt. The landowners' opposition to railways derived not only from their privacy being invaded but also from their objections to it as a form of transport. Lady Seafield said that she hated railways and that posting with four horses was the perfection of travelling.

The railway mania of the 1840s gave Scotland its main trunk system, and though many branch lines were added later it was this early nucleus which was of vital influence. As horse-drawn vehicles had competed for tourist traffic so did the trains, companies vying with one another to shorten the time of the journey. By 1888 London to Edinburgh took about eight hours, departing from King's Cross, while Euston offered the quickest route to Aberdeen and other places in the north of Scotland. The first sleeping car was built in 1873, two years after the refreshment basket, introduced by Messrs Spiers & Pond and now, unhappily, abandoned.

One blessing which rail travel conferred was that in order to be in time for the

Twelfth sportsmen no longer had to start as soon as Goodwood was over, but could race for the Cowes Town Cup or Yachtsman's Derby and still be in time for the opening day. For the journey from the house in London to the station a hansom cab—that most romantic of all forms of London transport, its beauty reflected in the pride its drivers took in their turnout—was the obvious vehicle. To the regular man-about-town the cabbies were old friends, each with his own nickname affectionately bestowed: Charles Old (Old & Bitter), Thomas Bacon (Porky), Charles Brown (Brown Upside Down), Robert Swannell (Old Black Lion Bob), William Speechley (Nicodemus), Robert Green (Old Greeny), James Tanner (Doctor), John Dew (Rhoderic Dhu). Travellers with heavy luggage would have had to engage a four-wheeler or growler for its conveyance, and they would have borne in mind that the railways levied extra charge on more than 150 lb for a 1st-Class passenger and 60 lb for 3rd-Class.

At the station a saloon carriage would have been booked consisting of three compartments, the centre being arranged as a sitting room, and those at either end for the ladies and the gentlemen of the party. Pillows, rugs, comfortable beds and gas lighting made for comfort, the larger pieces of luggage formed a table for dinner, and the provision of cold chicken curry, fruits and champagne were a satisfactory prelude to the night's sleep. But first it would have been necessary to ensure the safety of dogs and luggage. Then, as later, it was possible to break the regulations and take one or two of your favourite dogs with you, by slipping a suitable inducement into the hand of the attendant. For the dogs that travelled in the guard's van it was advisable to have zinc luggage labels attached to their collars, for everyone had heard of the Scottish porter who was in a dilemma with the brace of setters which had eaten off their addresses, and determined to send one down the line and the other up, while he dispatched the guncases to the station half-way between. Best of all was to transport dogs in wicker baskets which, in spite of the coachman's plea that they could not be carried on his conveyance, would be taken on to the lodge. Scottish kennels were notoriously ramshackle, and a dog's comfort could be ensured by using the travelling basket as a kennel, setting it off the ground with battens or stones and protecting top and sides with turf. Equal attention needed to be paid to the luggage; almost every box or portmanteau had a handle, yet, it was complained, these were the very last things a porter would lay hold of. He would prefer to haul on the straps and so damage them, carelessly fling a box on the ground regardless of the fragility of its contents, put a heavy piece of luggage on top of a camera or dump a box of 500 cartridges on a valuable dressing bag. A portion of the guard's van, it was recommended, should be set aside for guns and rods—jumbling them up with other

20 *Dunblane Station, Perthshire, in 1871: passengers changed here for the Callander and Oban line*

luggage resulted in broken stocks, damaged rifle sights and bent barrels.

And a cautionary word on the perils of leaving packing until the last moment never comes amiss. Thus Idstone, who had an unexpected summons to Perthshire, thrust what clothes he thought necessary into a portmanteau, filled a leather bag with boots and gaiters and rushed to catch the train. He squeezed himself into a full train, got cramp, and was made miserable by a plethoric old gentleman opposite who periodically refreshed himself with the breasts of cold chickens, French rolls and pale sherry while he starved in the corner. As Idstone reviewed the contents of his luggage he recollected that he had forgotten his loading rod (this was before the days of breech-loaders) and, worse than that, his double guncase had but one gun in it. The last straw was the discovery next day that he had packed the barrels of No. 2 and the stock of No. 1. As for clothes, he had made no more serious mistake than bringing a pair of odd gaiters, which led the keeper to ask if the gentleman who came last night had only one leg or two.

At last, as 8 p.m. drew near, all was ready. Porters had fled hither and thither, faint but pursuing, with piles of luggage which looked as if by no possibility would time or space permit of their going in the vans attached to the train. But the bustle was over now. The hands of the big clock were upon the hour. Mind had conquered matter; order had been established over chaos. The ticket inspectors stood clear. The guards made for particular door-handles; and, as the whistle screamed responsive to the waving green flag, the limited mail, with a dozen extra coaches to cater for the sporting rush, glided smoothly down the platform out of the big and gloomy station, *en route* for what the passengers thought the fairest country upon earth.

No messenger hurrying with a telegram could stop them now; this was no false start; they could feel the train gather speed as she went till she fairly flew down the line. Farewell, then, for three months to the worries and discomforts that assailed the London householder, though the young man of the party was looking rather solemn as he nestled back in the carriage cushions, and was thinking, maybe, that their flitting northwards, pleasant as it undoubtedly was, meant farewell, in his case, for three months to a pair of blue eyes that had looked somewhat lovingly into his own at recent dances.

If the emotion or excitement of the train inhibited courtship of sleep itself, 'it is pleasant to feel the pulsations of the great engine, like a living thing, as it forges its way ahead through the length of England. At last the wilds of Westmorland are reached, and the engine pants its way up the long incline to the Shap Summit, when one gets the first taste of the exhilarating mountain air. There is no need to look out of the windows to see your whereabouts if you know the line well; you can tell it by the gradient. The engine speaks to you in the night. The wheels of the carriage seem to labour out with difficulty an ever-recurrent phrase,[4] "I *think*-I-can; I *think*-I-can; I *think*-I-can." At times there is something human in it; again the vacant train follows the sound as it were some ditty played upon a jigging instrument. The Summit reached, the tune is varied and becomes a rapid and exultant paean, "I *thought* I could, I *thought* I could, I *thought* I could," which again quickly merges into a mere blind rush through the air, only periodically broken by the crash of the train passing through an arch as it tears its way down the hill towards Carlisle.'

At Carlisle a Caledonian engine would be attached to take the train across the border, up the long pull of Beattock and then at furious speed down the valley of the Clyde over to Stirling. Passengers for Argyll would change there to the Callander and Oban line, while those bound for Inverness would change at Perth to the Highland line.

21 The Game Cart *by Henry Alken. The ventilated compartments in the sides of the cart enabled dogs to be carried as well as game*

In the bustle of Perth station passengers would once more have to look to their luggage, or rather look for an obliging porter, for the latter breed was inclined to hint that while they did not mind a decent-sized carpet-bag or two, the furniture-removing business was entirely out of their line. A single passenger by train now carried as much personal luggage as a whole coachful did before steam took to the shafts. The single razor became a dressing-case, it was impossible to do without hip-baths, and the family poodle must also be taken as well as the favourite hearth-rug it chose to lie upon.

The baggage having been secured, the traveller of the '70s or '80s would have been hard put to get out of Perth station without being accosted by a speculator or dealer of some kind seeking out trade. There were stalwart gillies in kilts or homespun; amphibious fishermen, as much at home on the heather as with the herring nets; dealers in dogs, sanguine of palming off suspicious pointers and setters on innocent customers who had come north unprovided; and emissaries from enterprising tradespeople, eager to receive orders for stores.

The sensible thing to do was to head for the sanctuary of the 1st-Class refreshment room, where the specialities were the crimped salmon and sea-trout, inestimable finnans, rich cream and butter from the Carse of Gowrie and tea which, it was said, tasted as Bohea never tasted elsewhere. Thus fortified, stock could be taken of provisions, and in the event of some vital item having been forgotten, the situation could be remedied swiftly by recourse to all manner of tradesmen. Requirements in the field would be supplied by P. D. Malloch at 209 High Street, where fishing tackle, guns and all kinds of ammunition were stocked, or from Paton's gun shop, whence every evening cartridges were sent off to the moors. For the fortification of the inner man the Italian and Wine Warehouse respectfully begged attention to its wine cellars, reckoned to be the largest north of the Forth, as well as to its liqueurs, mineral waters, Indian and China teas, whiskies and brandies, coffee and chocolates. Due to inflation, however, Dupuy and Fils Epernay, who limited the sale of their produce to their old-established connection among the Nobility, Gentry and first-class Clubs, stated regrettably that they were compelled to price their 1874 Selected Grape champagne at 72s per dozen. If romance overtook the shooting party McIntyre & Stewart, Bread, Biscuit and Pastry Bakers, made marriage and christening cakes to order while, more mundanely but of more importance, William McKendrick, Family Butcher, would dispatch, neatly cut to order, tidily packed in hampers, by first available train to any station, lamb, veal, sweetbreads, kidneys, salt meat and tongues.

Finally, for transportation to the lodge, and for mobility during the holiday, horses and carriage could be hired for the season from the Perth Coach Hiring Establishment, who kept not only the best of horses and carriages but also civil, steady and careful coachmen.

Comfortable though the train journey may have been, as a means of travel it yielded in prestige to the private yachts owned by those who were fortunate enough to secure a moor on the coast with a good anchorage. Thereon hangs the tale of the pair of yachtsmen at Cowes who read, on 5 August, of a moor to let:

Craig-Na-Vrockan, Loch Eribol, Sutherland-Shire. Grouse (300 brace), black game, and snipe; lodge, comfortable though old fashioned; good anchorage, and would well suit a yachtsman, climate mild, the Gulf Stream flows under the windows. Rent, £250 the season, inclusive of services of Keeper and two dogs. Apply to Hume, Hamesucker, and McTavish, Writers to the Signet,

George Street, Edinburgh; or McDiarmaid and Jones, grouse-moor-mongers, Piccadilly, London.[5]

With guns and fishing tackle aboard, the regatta over and the yachts departing for Iceland, the fjords of Norway or Scottish anchorages, the two sportsmen wired the Scottish agents to secure the lease and an answer of acceptance duly arrived. The fact that a second answer soon followed saying that the place had been let that morning by the London agent to a Mr Soapstone of the yacht *Kestrel* at Cowes only increased the determination of Mr Templetrap and Mr Blackmarsh of the yacht *Kitty* to arrive first and seize possession. The *Kestrel* had nine hours' start on them, but they came in sight of her on 11 August. With no time to lose they launched a boat for the shore as soon as they could and fired two shots on the beach to claim possession. An irate keeper urged their arrest, but Mr Soapstone soon arranged a peaceful settlement, saying that he had only leased the lodge for his daughters and was not interested in shooting. All ended happily for the sportsmen, who secured not only the moor but in due course the hand in marriage of the two daughters as well.

CHAPTER 5

Highland Quarters

The first requisite for a grouse-shooter is patience; the next, a determination
to make himself comfortable under any circumstances—and to put up with any
inconveniences. *Thomas Oakleigh, 1837*

Before the era of the luxury shooting-lodge the visitor to the north might, if he was
well connected, enjoy the magnificent hospitality of Lord Huntly at Gordon
Castle and Glenfiddich Forest, of Lord Breadalbane at Taymouth Castle and
Black Mount, or of the Duke of Atholl at Blair Castle. Alternatively, as Highland
families were becoming keen to taste the pleasures of town life, he might find
someone willing to exchange houses for the term of the holiday. If a house in the
Highlands had no land attached to it the sportsman would not have to look far to
find a local landowner willing to let him roam his moors.

   The majority of those who rented grouse-shooting in the early Victorian era
had to content themselves with spartan conditions. Lord Kingston's shooting-
box, though in Ireland, no doubt had many counterparts in Scotland. It consisted
of a large parlour and two bedrooms; the beds were designed to fold up into large
armchairs, fitted with wheels, enabling them to be moved from room to room.
After the evening meal and superfluity of claret the occupants could sleep in them
without further disturbance, the servants having trundled them off into their
rooms and adapted them to the horizontal position.

   In remote areas, there was often no alternative to accepting the hospitality of a
shepherd or fox-hunter in his turf cabin. There the sportsman would find homely
fare and a good peat fire withal to warm himself. He would also have to endure
a smoky atmosphere and a leaking thatch over his bed if the rain fell too heavily.

   Such rugged conditions were more acceptable when a journey to a distant
shooting- or stalking-ground made return before nightfall to the lodge impossible.
Lord Malmesbury described how Sir James Hudson, British Minister in Turin,
spent a night in a shepherd's hut so that he could be out stalking early the
following day:

Sir James returned for dinner, having killed nothing, and gave a very amusing account of his night at the bothy. He said there were seven men, five dogs, three women, and a cat in two small rooms, more like hen coops than rooms, and only three beds for the whole party. The maid-of-all-work asked him with whom he would like to sleep, and he answered that if he couldn't sleep with her he would prefer Macoll, the stalker. The latter, however, replied, 'Methinks you had better sleep alone.'[1]

In early years, the comfort of some shepherd's cottage at least exceeded what most of the inns could provide. 'Such is the misery of the Highland public house,' wrote Colonel Peter Hawker in 1816, 'and particularly to our perfumed young men of fashion, that I have generally observed nine out of ten of them, however good may have been their sport, come home cursing and swearing most bitterly about their wooden berths, peat fires, and oatmeal cakes!'

The increasing flow of travellers led to improvements, yet it was often the remote inn which seldom welcomed a tourist and was beyond the range of commercial travellers which was best of all. A visitor was an event and cause of celebration, and though there was only a fire of peat and wood on the hearthstone under the capacious chimney, gargantuan feasts were roasted there. Sometimes an inn in the neighbourhood of moors was a nuisance to the landowners, and the sporting clientele an embarrassment to the innkeeper. Not everyone was discriminating on whose land they were shooting over. Meg Dodds observed with satisfaction that there was no guncase along with Francis Tyrel's baggage; 'for that weary gunning had brought him and her into trouble—the lairds had cried out upon it, as if she made her house a howff for common fowlers and poachers; and yet how could she hinder twa daft hempie callants from taking a start and an owerloup? They had been ower the neighbour's ground they had leave on up to the march, and they werena just to ken meiths when the moorfowl got up.'[2]

Such was the courtesy of the Scots that an inn was often resorted to by travellers only as a resting-place on a stage of their journey. When Osgood MacKenzie's father was told that an officer was staying at the local inn, an invitation was at once sent to him to lodge with the MacKenzie family. 'The idea of a gentleman . . . being allowed to remain at an inn was contrary to all rules of Highland hospitality and thought disgraceful.'[3] No doubt, too, it was a matter of local pride that the inns of a locality should be good. Charles St John described the inns on the Duke of Sutherland's property as clean, well kept, and the charges moderate, to a degree that the most suspicious and fastidious cockney traveller could find no fault with.

Those who pitched their expectations low in respect of Highland comfort were often pleasantly surprised. The bannocks of oats or barley, with goat's milk cheese and perhaps the unwonted luxury of braxy mutton from some sheep that had come to an untimely end tended to be the fare that was traditionally expected. Herbert Byng Hall who made a sporting tour of the Highlands in the 1840s, stayed at Meggernie Castle in Glenlyon, which quite changed his idea of a shooting-box, which 'had hitherto been limited to a species of mud hut placed on a wild and extensive moor', yet here he found everything he could wish for—short of luxury—in abundance.[4] He fared similarly elsewhere. At the Dalwhinnie inn the table offered a choice of well-flavoured heather-fed mutton, hotchpotch, fresh trout and salmon, poultry, game and the best of custard puddings. The whisky was excellent, as was the London porter brewed at St Andrews. The line of forts dating from General Wade's days could still be relied upon for welcome and comfort. The opening of the Caledonian Canal in 1822 had made the geographic position of Fort Augustus in particular as strategically apt for the traveller as it had been for the military. Whatever the merits of the Commandant as a soldier, he proved to be an admirable host.

Less fortunate men than Mr Byng Hall sometimes found that rented quarters fell short of advertised descriptions. A satirical novel of Thomas Jeans, *The Tommiebeg Shootings*, describes delightfully the perils that could befall a greenhorn. Samuel Brixey had been a partner in the well-known mercantile firm of Brixey Brothers, Liverpool. His retirement in London was spent quietly with his sister, his only journeys from home being the occasional outing with a couple of friends to Thames Ditton or Hampton for a day's punt-fishing during the gudgeon season. The attractions of a sporting holiday in Scotland aroused Mr Brixey

23 *By the 1880s, the family holiday on the moors was fashionable, although few lodges had a bathroom*

24 *London merchants competed with their counterparts in the north of England and Scotland in providing everything a sportsman might need*
25 *By the early 20th century, the family grocer in the Highlands usually stocked a wide variety of luxury and practical items in his whisky-perfumed store*

after he had suffered an attack of influenza. His doctor, McPhun, advised him to take a moor so that he could get some bracing air, and sent him a few books such as St John's *Highland Sports*, Scrope's *Days of Deerstalking* and Hugh Snowie's list of moors to be let. Snowie's document whetted his appetite with its variety of places to offer and advantages of each. Red and roe deer, grouse, ptarmigan, black grouse, hares, rabbits, partridges, woodcock, snipe and duck appeared to be as plentiful as blackberries. But there was one that appeared to combine every desirable quality. The advertisement read as follows:

Shootings and Fishings in Inverness-shire

The shootings and fishings of Tommiebeg, extending over the grounds of Knockandown, and marching with the deer forest of Corriewhiskie and Glenfaulachin, embracing a range over from 12,000 to 15,000 acres, or thereby. The shootings are quite first-rate. Red and roe deer frequently on the ground. Every variety of game—grouse, ptarmigan and black game on the upper range, and the low ground abounds in partridges, hares, rabbits—with woodcock, snipe and wildfowl in the season. The river affords trout fishing and salmon after rain. Excellent salmon fishing to be had in the Spey, which abounds the property. Not more than 800 brace of grouse to be killed in the season and ten deer, that is to say seven stags and three hinds. The lodge, furnished with all modern conveniences, is situated in an extensive park and contains one public-room, three bedrooms, kitchen, and a sleeping room for gillies. Intending offerors may apply for further particulars to Mr Evan McSnail, Morayburgh; or to Alexander Worriecow, Esq., W.S., Edinburgh.

In due course a lease of the moor was secured and Brixey set off in the company of his young friend and ward, Peter Fribbles. A brace of dud pointers was purchased for the sum of £20 from a dishonest dog-dealer, and the party was completed by the presence of Captain Downey, whose life was devoted to foisting himself upon the unwary for the purpose of getting the best of sport at no cost to himself.

Prior to occupation of the lodge at Tommiebeg the party stayed at the near-by inn at Morayburgh and called on Evan McSnail the factor. They learned from him, to their surprise, that the lodge contained no furniture. This had been sold the year before and McSnail had bought it all back for, as he put it, the convenience of the next incomer. The sum they were asked to pay in rent was, unbeknown to them, no less than what he had paid for the whole lot outright. But a bargain was eventually struck and next day the dogcart set off in advance with all the necessary impedimenta. Some dozens of Prestonpans beer, sundry samples of wine, whisky, a large box of groceries, tea and sugar, coffee and chocolate, sauces and soap, candles and curry powder, mixed pickles, pepper and salt, mustard and marmalade as well as an imposing case containing a ham, a side of bacon, and two or three tongues and other comestibles.

As the three sportsmen set out for Tommiebeg the next day in the rain their spirits were high as they pondered on the fact that the method of keeping out the gently insinuating damp of a Scotch mist, of steering balloons against the wind, of squaring a circle, and of concocting a faultless budget were problems yet to be worked out. The pleasures of anticipation contrasted starkly with their emotion on arrival. The sight that greeted them was a rude-looking square building of rough unpointed masonry about a quarter of a mile from the road, round which a low wall of stones, picked off the surface, and piled up one upon the other, formed an irregularly shaped enclosure. So desolate was the spot, especially when seen under such unfavourable circumstances, that it seemed hardly possible that anyone could have fixed on such a site for a dwelling and the travellers were only awakened to the melancholy reality, of its being actually the lodge which was to be their habitation, by the carriage turning suddenly into a rough track leading towards it.

Both Brixey and Fribbles had let their imaginations run optimistically on the qualities of the lodge. Fribbles pictured it from the advertisement, situated in an extensive park, the dwelling itself being something in the 'Camberwell Gothic' or the 'Decorated Brixton' style of architecture. He had seen park lodges, and it had often struck him how nice and comfortable they always appeared to be. He had decided that the ancient mansion of Tommiebeg might have been pulled down at some time, and the lodge fitted up as a residence by the probable addition of a new drawing-room or dining-room. The clumps of trees judiciously dispersed; a noble avenue of elm or beech along the carriage drive leading up to the site of the old manor house; a fine sheet of water, with a swan and a boat-house to match; a herd of deer (out of which they were by agreement allowed to shoot ten head), scattered about in groups, cropping the tender herbage, or reposing in the leafy covert. The reality disillusioned them all, but when the furniture had been installed, baggage unpacked and a good peat fire lit the house assumed an air of reasonable comfort.

It was true, of course, that the purpose of a shooting-lodge was to be conveniently situated for shooting, but the compatibility of beauty, comfort and convenience could have been achieved more often than it was. Anthony Trollope described in *The Duke's Children* an unsuccessful example, Crummie-Toddie:

> The lodge itself was as ugly as a house could be, white, of two stories, with the door in the middle and windows on each side, with a slate roof and without a tree near it. It was in the middle of the shooting, and did not create a town around itself as do sumptuous mansions, to the great detriment of that seclusion which is favourable to game. 'Look at Killancodlem,' Dobbes had been heard to say—'a very fine house for ladies to flirt in; but if you find a deer within six miles of it I will eat him first and shoot him afterwards.' There was a spartan simplicity about Crummie-Toddie which pleased the spartan mind of Reginald Dobbes.
> 'Ugly, do you call it?'
> 'Infernally ugly,' said Lord Gerald.
> 'What did you expect to find. A big hotel, and a lot of cockneys? If you come after grouse, you must come to what the grouse think pretty.'[5]

Whatever the older generation felt about it, the holiday *en famille* on the moors was the fashionable thing by the 1880s and Highland lairds, enriched by high shooting rents, were vying with one another in building lodges equipped to emulate the comforts of the finest homes. Tradesmen, eager for Sassenach silver and keen to avoid the former necessity of a Scottish expedition bringing its supplies from the south, stocked the most elegant of trifles as well as the everyday things of life. Even the Tommiebeg shooters, in the middle of the century, found the rural merchant a complete Jack-of-all-trades. There was nothing they could ask for, from parasols to powder-flasks, that he could not furnish. Hats and bonnets, male and female greatcoats and petticoats, bottles of ink and bottles of whisky, pens and perfumery, tapioca and tape, creels and crockery, mulls and macintoshes, pigtails and plaids, tin-tacks and toasting-forks, groceries and gunpowder, cheeses and checked aprons, saucepans and soap, crinoline and cobbler's wax, tallow candles and treacle, fusees and fire-irons, mousetraps and mustard-pots, buttons and blacking, spectacles and Spanish licorice, were a few of the items stocked in his whisky-perfumed store.

As in all things, there was regret for the old way of life; for the but and ben with its white harling that beamed a welcome; for the gathering of driftwood at the riverside to raise a fire for breakfast, for the header into the cold waters of the loch to set one up for the business of the day. Accommodation may have been cramped, furniture sparse, and in wet weather the atmosphere claustrophobic, but when the sun shone it had its snug charms.

The desire for something better, more suitable for a leisurely family holiday, was fostered by the publicity given to northern sport by the pen of William Scrope in *Days of Deerstalking* and by the fashionable brush of Sir Edwin Landseer. As for the initiative of the landlords, or lack of it, in providing better accommodation, *The Tommiebeg Shootings* came as a guncrack. The very title of the book was anathema, but initial rage gave way to shame and improvements went steadily forward. To Thomas Jeans, more than to any other Victorian author, can be ascribed the influence of bringing home to laird and factor alike that it was in their interests to see that the customer got what he wanted. Moreover, the landlords were fortunately in a position to gain ready access to bank credit. It was a general belief that the improvement of agriculture rather than industrial investment was the first charge on the capital resources of a landlord, and it was only natural that this should be reflected in the building of prestigious mansions.

The pursuit of comfort sometimes went too far; the aims and graces of a Belgravian mansion in the heart of the Highlands could be wearisome, and one sympathises with the man who became so tired of his stay that he wired to a friend to wire for him to come home at once on urgent business.

Few people would wish or would be able nowadays to emulate the Victorians in their shooting-lodges on the matter of food and wine, but other amenities which would be regarded nowadays as necessities were almost non-existent. Few lodges boasted a bathroom, though hip-baths were plentiful. Absence of running water would not have been considered roughing it, for the young bloods who visited Scotland were brought up to it. There was, for example, not a single bathroom at Eton, and even King Edward VII sometimes took his own bath with him when he visited his friends. It was only after the First World War that, partly because of the need for labour saving, bathrooms and electric light began to be installed. Another invention, the motor car, came into general use after the Boer War and led to a welcome improvement in access roads between lodges and shooting-grounds. Previously, it had been the custom on extensive estates to convey the shooting-party to their beat by brake or wagonette, and even then the absence of roads frequently entailed an exhausting walk.

In the course of one generation the grouse-shooting holiday had been transformed from an all-male expedition to a fashionable social gathering. Old men like Augustus Grimble may have regretted the new trappings of luxury, but surely even he would have preferred female company to his own experience at the Bettyhill Inn where, on one occasion, he found himself sole guest, not a newspaper in the place, and the three books boasted by the house bearing the titles *Early Graves, Elijah and Ahab* and *A Candle Lighted By The Lord*.

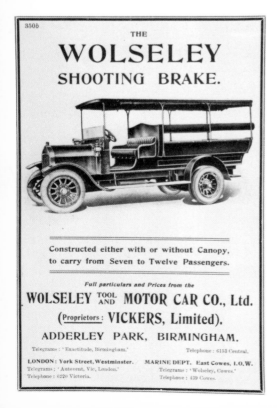

26 *The motor car came into use after the Boer War and helped to improve access roads between lodges and shooting-grounds*

PART THREE

The Chase

CHAPTER 6

The Noble Grouse

'We *are* a queer race,' mused Charles, lighting another cigarette. 'Nobody ever understood what Wilde meant when he wrote: "Yet each man kills the thing he loves." But we
bring up millions of grouse and partridges and pheasants solely in order to amuse our-
selves by killing them, and all the time we write and talk of our victims, and have pictures
painted of them in their last moments, with a wealth of sentimental fellow-feeling, in
which no trace of our intended or actual treachery to them ever appears.' *J. K. Stanford*,
The Twelfth, *1944*

In times past the red grouse has enjoyed several names, local in origin depending
on whether the native country has been England, Ireland or Scotland. Notable
among these are moorfowl or muirfowl, moorgame and moorcock, gorcock and
heather-hen. The word grouse is itself the only foreign thing about it, deriving
probably from an old French adjective *griesche*, signifying grey or speckled. The
plural word grice, singular grows, applying to the black grouse or black game,
first appears in an ordinance of Henry VIII dated 1531, and though Gaelic
names have been conjured up by scholars and pieced together to comprise the
word grouse it is probable that the French derivation is the correct one.

When one considers that grouse moors cover 3 million acres of Scotland, nearly
1 million acres of England and Wales and 1 million acres of Ireland, it is not
surprising that the well-being of the grouse has long been linked with the prosperity of moorland communities. Where there is a failure of grouse the livelihood of a
number of country people can either be put in jeopardy or welcome supplemen-
tary income forfeited. That fact has long been recognised, and until recently
grouse disease, namely strongylosis, was believed to be the principal cause of a
depleted grouse population. The supposed importance of the disease prompted
the Grouse Disease Inquiry Committee which, under the chairmanship of Lord
Lovat, reported in 1911 with a monumental scientific work running to 650 pages.
Much of the text and many of the illustrations were done by Edward Wilson, who
later perished with Scott in the Antarctic.

Knowledge of grouse behaviour has advanced rapidly in recent years, prin-

Hen red grouse and eggs

cipally thanks to the inquiry set up in 1956, which was a consequence of the dwindling of grouse stocks in the late 1930s and a subsequent failure of recovery. This inquiry was set up by the Scottish Landowners' Federation at Banchory and was later embodied in a Nature Conservancy Research Station. One of the most striking conclusions was that strongylosis is not a paramount factor in causing a decline of grouse, but to understand the varied dangers which grouse are subject to it is necessary to study their life cycle.

Grouse-shooting ceases by law on 10 December, but only a few hardy people brave the winter weather to venture out after the end of October. The season of the predation of man is short, but the grouse that survives the guns of autumn has other predators to evade and dangers to overcome if it is to survive into another spring.

The approach of winter brings competition for breeding territory; even the old birds with territories this year will have to compete for their own ground again, and this rivalry takes toll of more lives than anything else. The bird that fails to find a home faces probable death through starvation, and the proportion so lost ranges up to 50 per cent each year. This wastage underlines the importance of hard shooting early in the season so that the requisite number of birds may be culled. On a moor where the population is high it may be necessary to kill almost half the stock to avoid overpopulation, and if shooting is left until the early winter the deterioration of weather may inhibit an adequate cull.

There was a roar like thunder of over three thousand wings as the grouse leapt simultaneously from the heather. As John Tye said later to a crony in the Sweatenham Arms: 'The moor fair riz at us and come ascreechen. Them birds properly bid us defiance! That was like all the geese getting up on Holkham Sands.' Dugald, who had not ceased to believe that the moor was bewitched, felt as if every grouse in Aberdeenshire was bearing down on him. (J. K. Stanford, *The Twelfth*, p. 80.)

Birds of both sexes which fail either to get territories or to pair, form into packs once the wild weather starts, usually in September and October. No doubt some members of the pack pair subsequently, but this surplus population is a nuisance on moors where an adequate cull has not yet been made.

The plant on which the grouse is so heavily dependent for its well-being is *Calluna vulgaris*, common ling heather. When heather fails, grouse fail. That is not to say that the tender shoots of heather form the sole diet; cornfields, particularly oats, are resorted to commonly, and turnip leaves, bramble, hawthorn and rowan will be used as food. It is no coincidence that the best grouse moors border on

28 *Common ling heather* (Calluna vulgaris)*; grouse eat the shoots*

agricultural land, for there the moorland diet can be supplemented, particularly if the winter is hard. On their own ground they enjoy a diet enhanced with the indigenous berries, such as blaeberry, cranberry and cloudberry. When these are ripe the birds migrate to the high ground for the seasonal feasting.

Two necessary items of sustenance are water and grit. The former is always present to some degree, and even on hot summer mornings there is usually some dew. Nevertheless, a moor that is well supplied with burns that do not run dry will

29 *Hen red grouse and chicks*

sustain a better grouse population than one that is without them. Natural grit is usually present in abundance, either in the beds of burns or on the hilltops and in the peat bogs. Moorland roads are a favourite place for grouse to grit, and this is truer today than in times past, for many new roads have been made for easier access or to enable forestry operations to be carried out. The person who wishes to **watch grouse at close quarters** should motor along an unmetalled hill road, for they will take little notice of the car. The purpose of grit is to aid the digestion of heather fibre in the gizzard, and it will be retained in the gizzard for some weeks if fresh grit is unobtainable. The old grit, which will have become polished in the process of grinding food, is eventually emitted and fresh, abrasive grit is eaten. It is always wise to supplement natural grit by scattering small piles of purchased grit as widely as possible about the moor, and this applies particularly before the onset of winter. In that season the coarser nature of the heather takes more milling to break it down into digestible food.

The fact that grouse need more food in winter than at other times of the year is a critical factor, and therefore a moor which has good heather in winter months enjoys an advantage. If there is a threat of starvation, inherent on an over-populated moor with insufficient territories and threatened by a fierce winter the fascinating enigma of migration may occur. On the whole movements are small and local, occurring when food and water are sought. Longer journeys may take place when birds are driven by beaters or disturbed by a predator such as an eagle. The dramatic sight of a huge pack in flight, apparently bent on a long journey, is usually caused by the presence of a bird of prey. As one covey flees others join it and so the numbers swell.

Snow will cause temporary desertion of a moor. When deep snow covers the high ground birds will move downhill, and conversely they will move uphill when deep snow at low altitudes does not drift. On high ground the wind will usually blow some of the heather clear. Prolonged snow may cause temporary migration for three or four miles for a month or two, but grouse will normally return to their old home.

If one accepts the fact that normally grouse only migrate under stress of one kind or another, and then only over a relatively short distance, the fact remains that long flights do occur and the ultimate destination, or intended destination, of the birds concerned, is hard to understand. Individual cases are difficult to auth-enticate, but cited instances of unusual behaviour are so numerous that they cannot be dismissed as evidence. A few examples may be of interest. About 1865 the tenant of the island of Gigha shot about ninety brace; since no grouse bred on the island, presumably the problem of space accounted for birds moving from the mainland. In the severe winter of 1878–9 a pack of grouse was seen crossing the Moray Firth in December, making for the Banff coast. Much snow was lying at the time in east Sutherland and Caithness. In September 1885 a grouse was shot on the Mendips and it was suggested that it crossed over the Bristol Channel, migrating from Breconshire. From time to time fishermen have drawn up grouse in their trawl nets, and in December 1917, at least thirty miles east of Lerwick, a covey of grouse flew on board H.M. destroyer *Ophelia* and settled on deck.

To cite a more recent example, Frank Gillan, formerly head keeper to the late Duke of Sutherland, witnessed thousands of grouse congregated in Strathfleet, Dunrobin Glen, Strath Brora and Kildonan in the early spring of 1955. They were sitting on a hill facing the sea, apparently driven there by a strong north wind and kept on the move by an eagle on their tail. Stress once more, but the interesting thing was that neighbouring moors which until that time were well stocked had hardly any birds in the seasons of 1955 and 1956. There were no other apparent factors present to reduce the grouse population drastically, so what happened to them?

Observations on the wandering habits of individual grouse have been made in several instances where a physical peculiarity of the bird has made identification possible. The Committee of 1911 cited a pure white grouse in Ayrshire that was shot at on Glencairn and Upper Cree, was subsequently shot at twelve miles away and was finally killed by a keeper nine miles away from either of these moors. A sceptic might say that because of its freak colour it became alienated from its kind and was therefore compelled to wander, but it leaves an open question. There is no doubt that grouse are able to travel long distances and to orientate themselves in the correct direction, as has been proved in several cases where tame birds have been removed from their native place and have returned, sometimes over more than a hundred miles. When so tamed they become positively cheeky. J. G. Millais[1] described a bird which would even accompany shooters to the hill and was so outraged at being 'pointed' at by a dog that it attacked it. Characteristics such as these defy generalisation, and if there is still mystery attached to the movement or migration of grouse it only enhances their fascination. When the movement of grouse appears to be a mystery, one is tempted to believe that the ghost of George Hysteron-Proteron haunts the moor.

The birds that survive the winter will begin to pair and to fight when the weather softens, even as early as January if the weather is mild. The cocks fight one another with the bill, springing into the air, worrying one another, beating each other with their wings. The victor rises in vertical flight with a crow of triumph, while the captured lady remains submissive beside him. Soon another male will challenge, and the performance will be repeated.

With the coming of spring the cock begins his display, strutting stiffly and proudly, neck held high, tail cocked. He will pursue the hen, the pair flying low and fast over the ground, twisting and turning, perhaps alighting on alien territory, to the aggressive fury of the male incumbent. The latter will not only drive off the intruding cock but may well woo successfully his lady. Occasionally a prosperous moor will sustain cocks with two hens, though monogamy is more usual.

Now is the time when the hen grouse must be in good condition to withstand whatever risks bad weather may bring. If she is in poor physical shape she will lay fewer eggs than normal, and she and her chicks will suffer if frost and east winds wither the heather shoots. Snow may be an ally, for it will cloak the heather from the worst of the frost damage. The hen herself will continue to sit tenaciously through bad weather, even to the extent of being covered with snow herself, and perhaps perishing. Sometimes she will wait until the snow has melted and then she will commence brooding. If an intruder approaches the cock will fly right away, while the hen will flutter away over the heather, trying to mislead the enemy. The eggs are as resilient as the bird that lays them, for they will endure up to about 15°F of frost when pheasant eggs would be rendered useless.

The nesting site will be in longish heather, but with a good all-round view and with easy access to short heather for good feeding. Dry ground is chosen, and if the nest should become waterlogged the hen will desert quite readily. The nest is prepared by the hen, and a clear view from it will be compatible with sufficient heather to screen it from aerial enemies. The lining is meagre, composed of a little vegetation, perhaps a few feathers. Eggs are laid between March and the end of April within a period of twenty-four to forty-eight hours of each other and incubation is about twenty-two days. The clutch normally comprises seven or eight eggs, which are of a pale olive colour, blotched with a darkish reddy brown. They are well concealed from predators, for they match the background of moss, lichen, peat and heather stems.

The nesting season coincides with the end of heather burning. By law heather may be burned from 1 October to 15 April, and in a wet spring extension can be obtained until 30 April. This may seem a long and adequate time for the appropriate acreage to be burned, but the days when the ground is sufficiently dry are few. The man who is tempted by dry weather to burn after the middle of April is unwise, for he will destroy many nests. As to whether either autumn or spring burning is more beneficial, there are divided opinions, but it should be done at any time possible, for there are too few dry days in most years to accomplish what is necessary.

The task of heather burning is a skilled one. A good grouse moor is a good sheep hill, but unfortunately many shepherds are keen to burn large tracts of heather, and this accords ill with the territorial requirements of grouse. In order that different pairs of grouse can have access to a variety of heather in different stages of growth, the best plan is to burn in strips about thirty-five yards wide. A burning rotation of twelve to fifteen years should be maintained, and hence it is impossible on any but a very small moor to achieve the ideal of burning patches of about one acre. The ground must not be too dry for burning, else the fire will be so fierce and thorough the heather seed on the ground will be destroyed and grass or bracken will establish themselves. A steady breeze blowing over the moor will ensure the

30 *A keeper watches heather burning; by law, heather may be burned from 1 October to 15 April*

fire's swift progress and, although the burnt area may look untidy with unburnt heather stalks, the surface of the ground will be unharmed. If the soil is thin erosion can take place and the ground become barren of vegetation. By contrast, a fire in very dry weather may be carried underground among the peat hags and burn for weeks.

To achieve the ideal pattern of different stages of heather growth, each year areas to be burned must be plotted carefully in relation to what has been done in previous years. Tactics must also be worked out to take into account different wind directions. A fire that runs out of control will destroy the work of years, and therefore it is essential to run the fire towards a natural barrier such as a burn or rushy hollow. Sometimes a sudden change of wind can send the best laid plans awry, and the team of men who beat out the fire must be adequate in numbers.

Bracken is a menace that must be constantly controlled. It always encroaches on the best land, it harbours predators, and in the vicinity of butts it seems to

31 *Heather burn pattern over a grouse moor, well done in small patches*

inhibit the scenting ability of retrievers when birds fall into it. Ticks breed readily in bracken, causing the death of both sheep and grouse, the latter by infection with coccidiosis. The time-honoured method of destroying bracken is to cut the young plant twice, in May and June, when a curl is seen on the stem. If this is done for three or four years it is completely effective, but in these days of high labour costs it is an expensive method. In recent years a chemical spray has been developed which, applied through a lightweight battery-operated hand sprayer, can treat relatively large and inaccessible areas efficiently.

One of the most difficult moorland pests to control is the heather beetle, *Lochmaea suturalis*. Little attention was paid to the beetle before the 1911 Grouse Inquiry, because it was not recognised, and it was not until the mid-1930s, when outbreaks became more intense each year, that serious study was made of it. The effect of the beetle on an area of heather is to make it appear frosted, which is what the trouble was at first thought to be. Heather is attacked by beetle larvae in July

32 *The heather beetle* (Lochmaea suturalis), *one of the most difficult moorland pests to control. Heather is attacked by beetle larvae in July and August. An illustration by Edward Wilson from* The Grouse in Health and in Disease *(1911). Actual dimension is shown by the vertical line above*

and August, when the leaves and stems appear ruddy in colour, caused by the stripping off of bark. Plants up to ten years' old can generally withstand the attack, but older heather is liable to succumb. The eggs require a humid environment for their development and are laid chiefly on sphagnum moss. Boggy moorland is therefore most susceptible to attack, and as burning cannot be done in the summer months, drainage is the only positive form of control.

Nowadays mechanised drainage is a relatively easy task compared to the hand drainage which used to be carried out before the Second World War, largely by Irish labourers. The only drawback is that modern drains tend to slope insufficiently at the edges and are too deep. Grouse love to search in drains for seeds and grit, and a chick which falls into a drain cannot get out easily.

Fortunately chicks, in the face of all these hazards, are as hardy as their mother, able to run about almost immediately they hatch. The vigilant and aggressive mother watches over them carefully, and she will attack a dog or a hawk, and will even fly at a human being, only swerving away at the last moment. In the first two or three weeks of their life the diet of the young grouse consists largely of insects. Flies, spiders, chrysalises and slugs are all eaten, as well as plant foods. A dearth of insect life caused by a dry and cold spring can therefore be fatal to them. The necessary abundance of insects is aided by the presence of other animals on a moor, such as sheep, cattle, hares and deer, for insects feed on their droppings. In winter the larger animals serve another useful purpose in breaking up the layers of snow with their feet and so enabling grouse to get at the heather.

At about a week old the chicks are feeding chiefly on heather. Maturity comes fast, and the tiny creature born in May, with its yellowish down, barred and blotched with black about its head and chest, becomes indistinguishable at a cursory glance from its parents in September. By that time too, the hen and the cock may be identified, the latter having a comb of a brighter hue of red and his plumage a deeper, richer bronze. The colour nevertheless may be of several variations, according to geography and environment. J. G. Millais analysed them in some detail and in summary classed them as the red, black and white-spotted varieties.

Of the diseases from which grouse suffer, the most notorious is strongylosis or, as it is colloquially known, grouse disease. Most grouse carry some strongyle worms, and it is natural that birds in poor condition will be more seriously infested than those in good condition. As the strongyle worm is only detectable with the aid of a magnifying glass or microscope, death is often erroneously attributed to the

33 Old Grouse on the Tops *by Thorburn. Reproduced from* The Grouse (*see plate 87*)

34 The Home of the Red Grouse *by Thorburn. On the high moors*

Grouse Flighting to the Stooks (c. *1900*) *by Thorburn. Flights to valleys at harvest are an* *ntial part of the feeding pattern*

36 Walking-up Grouse (*1893*) by Edward Neale (*op. 1850–1910*). *Grit aids digestion of heather fibre in the gizzard*

disease. Like the tick, however, it is a debilitating factor, encouraging virus diseases to thrive and kill the victim.

As spring and summer progress the moorland keeper waits anxiously for the signs of success or failure of breeding. By early July the shepherds, who will have gathered the hill for the sheep clipping, will be able to give him a good idea from the broods of grouse they and their dogs have flushed of how successful the hatch has been. If the omens are good, he will feel satisfaction as at dawn he watches the sun come up over the hill and he listens to the sounds of the bird whose welfare he has so assiduously sought, but with far less certainty than the mere hatcher of pheasant or partridge eggs. The most muted call is from the hen, described imaginatively by one writer as 'yap, yap, yap, yore, yore, yore' and a low whining noise like the wheel of a barrow that wants oiling. The more extrovert cock advertises himself with a spring in the air and a 'cuck, cuck, ura-r-r-r-r'. Most distinct of all, recognisable by anyone who has never heard it before but has read about it, is his 'Go Back, Go Back, Go Back'. That is the signature tune of the grouse.

CHAPTER 7

Dogs

I have no ambition to see my name in the county newspapers as having
bagged my seventy brace of grouse, in a certain number of hours, on such and such a hill.
Charles St John, 1845

The origins of the pointing or setting dog are obscure. The pointer derived from a
cross between the Spanish pointer and a foxhound, the latter adding speed, and
both pointers and setters had spaniel ancestry. At one time the setter was known
as the English spaniel, and hence in Scott's *The Antiquary*, we find Hector praising
his 'spaniel' for her 'travel', i.e., pace and range. A breed of spaniel developed into
the setter as we know it today, being adapted to its new role as changes occurred
in methods of sport. Modern breed names reflect original purpose. In the days
when game was customarily taken with nets spaniels were divided into two
classes; one, the larger, was taught to sit or set for the purpose of allowing the net
to be drawn over the covey of crouching partridges or grouse, while the smaller
dog, the springer, found and sprung the game. The smaller type retained, of
course, its role, the gun merely being substituted for the net as the instrument of
capture. Only towards the end of the Victorian era, when large bags of game
necessitated quicker retrievers, did the labrador, which came to this country
originally in 1853, gradually eclipse the spaniel.

The history of gundogs is thus closely linked to the development of firearms
because the muzzleloading gun, limited by its slow rate of fire, did not lend itself
to the practice of driving game. By contrast, it was in complete harmony with the
work of the dog; the command 'Down charge' has long since lost its use in kennel
vocabulary, when the lengthy process of reloading after a shot enabled the dog to
recover its wind. Lack of consideration for the dogs was one of the criticisms
levelled at the advocates of breechloaders.

The common practice of shooting grouse over dogs lasted longer than it otherwise would have done because the innate conservatism of sportsmen made them
reluctant to change to breechloaders even when, by the 1860s, they were a proven

success. Extra weight, more likelihood of mechanical failure, heavy recoil and the burden of carrying heavy cartridges, were all reasons cited for rejecting the breechloader, and it was not until about the 1880s, when ejecting mechanisms were in use, that general acceptance took place. It is surprising that as late as 1887 the view was expressed in the Badminton Library volume on shooting that the ejector was of little practical use because the gun became so hot that no advantage could be gained. It is fair to add in support of the old school of sportsmen, that in the deliberate form of shooting practised over dogs they took pride in either killing or missing, and that the rapid shooting which patent ejectors encouraged also encouraged less care and shots at impossible ranges.

So, the shooter of that era set out for the hill wearing a chimney-pot hat (soft, felt hats were attributes of the lower orders) and a cloth coat, breeches and gaiters. The best coat boasted the most pockets. The loading rod would be suspended through a pipe attached to a belt which crossed the back on one side, while the shot pouch crossed the other shoulder. The right-hand upper pocket held wadding, the lower pocket the flask, and the other pockets were encumbered with nipple wrenches, screwdrivers and the general repertoire of the amateur armourer. Only by about 1870 did the coat, of necessity, become simpler, and tweed suits of matching jacket and knickerbocker trousers become fashionable.

Elsewhere, in my chapter on the life of a grouse, I have spoken of heather burning, but it is important to emphasise that, historically, different phases in heather management had bearing on the period when pointers and setters reigned supreme and when, subsequently, driving became fashionable. In the pre-Victorian, and in the early part of the Victorian era, as shooting increased in popularity, which meant shooting over dogs, the management of heather was conducted as seemed best, and as it turned out erroneously for birds to sit to the dog. Up to about 1850, when sheep were still an important feature of the moorland economy, burning was generally done by shepherds. It was a rough-and-ready business, but the principle of burning a tenth of the moor each year was generally adhered to, and in consequence grouse stocks, judging from occasional bags recorded, were high. As shooting became ever more fashionable, control of burning fell to the keeper and he, anxious to preserve large tracts of long heather where birds would lie close till the shooters were within gunshot distance, burned no heather at all. This period may be dated roughly between 1850 and 1873. The disastrous disease epidemic which struck grouse about 1873 coincided with the Game Laws Commission which was investigating the relationship between sporting and farming interests, and it was a notable feature of evidence given to the Commission that farmers who leased the sporting rights of their farms burned

37 The Twelfth of August *by George Straton Ferrier (?–1912)*

large areas of heather to get the land back into proper rotation for sheep and enjoyed doubled or trebled bags of grouse. The lesson of rotational burning was being learned and on the richer type of moorland the necessity of driving grouse to achieve a proper cull was realised.

The prudent sportsman of the earlier years would ensure that he had suitable dogs before leaving for the north. It was usually necessary to take them with him, because there were few in Scotland, and after the grouse season they were brought south again for partridge-shooting or, indeed, went to the overseas market, to point quail in Indiana or snipe in Russia. The scarcity of good dogs in Scotland reflected also Scots keepers' alleged inability to handle well. In an earlier generation Colonel Thornton remarked that 'no man can have any species of dog clever without some sort of pains, and in general they neglect them in Scotland'. The surest way to get good dogs was to purchase them privately or at the sales of well-known sportsmen's surplus stocks, which were mostly held at Aldridge's in St Martin's Lane, London, in the early part of the summer. To hire dogs the normal

38 The First Right and Left *by Thorburn. A Gordon setter on point*

charge was 16 guineas a brace for the whole season or part of the season only, the lessee paying for the keep of the dogs during the time he had them in his possession. Caution had to be exercised in dealing with dog-breakers, who displayed their kennel on their own premises. The dogs would drop at the sound of a pistol and perhaps get a point or two at tame birds, but inability to find game, quarter the ground and obey signals could not be detected. John Colquhoun's advice on buying a dog is as sound as ever today. Rather than pay an immense price for a distinguished pedigree from a celebrated dealer, procure a pup of the best dog and bitch in your own neighbourhood. The best pointer he ever had was bred from a sire and dam unknown to any but local fame. The finest setter he ever possessed was bought for £12 from an obscure kennel.

The question of breed must always be one of personal preference, but if it is looked at objectively few would take issue with Colquhoun's opinion that the pointer was best. He found it a more docile and pleasant dog to shoot over than the setter, but if the sportsman had a scanty kennel he would recommend setters, as they were capable of enduring more fatigue and were not so apt to be footsore. W. A. Adams maintained that setters withstood the cold better than pointers, otherwise he had no preference. He warned, however, against the show bench and field trial strains, and his words continue to echo in sporting circles today. On the show bench, he said, it was not pretended for one moment that any good accrued in a sporting sense; all was sacrificed to shape, size and coat, which was fine if you had it in a sporting dog but probably you had to do without some qualities if you were to have brains and keenness. Napoleon, Wellington and General Sheridan were all small men, and their physique would not have commanded prizes on the show bench.

As for field trial dogs, Adams asserted that they were rarely useful for sport. At a field trial a bold, pretentious dog was wanted that would go in and do just one or two things in a certain way; whether he was an industrious and good worker was a matter of indifference. A really good dog, if a little shied by the crowd round him, would be quite out of the running in a field trial. However, there was no doubt that field trial dogs possessed high qualities that were useful as a cross in breeding.

Adams appreciated that virtue to the point of faultlessness can be very boring, and that the most enjoyable dogs to shoot over are those which display independence of character. Witness Shot, Osgood MacKenzie's curly retriever which he took with him to the hill in August 1855 to try to shoot his first grouse, armed with a little 3-lb gun and a licence to shoot game:

39 Well Found and Well Backed *by Thorburn. A brace of English setters on point*

All we and Shot found in the open were two coveys . . . a pair of grouse with one cheeper, which Shot promptly caught in his big ugly mouth, and another pair with two young birds, out of which small lot I contrived to shoot the old cock as he ran in front of me. [In search of black game:] . . . Shot was not long in finding one of the coveys Big Sandy of the Geese had told us of. Up they got in ones and twos, fat young cocks, with their plumage half black and half brown. I blazed at them more than once, but was so excited that I felt sure I could not have hit anything. However, Shot . . . tore after them, and soon returned with a fine young black-cock in his mouth; of course, it was supposed I must have wounded him, though there were no signs of any pellets. The next covey Shot put up out of range of my poor little scatter gun, but notwithstanding, he brought back another young beauty and laid it at our feet. It seemed as if my firing or not was quite a matter of indifference to Shot. As for blue hares, even a well-grown leveret had not a chance if Shot got a sight of it, unless it went to ground, and then he would come and ask us to help him to dig it out. If ever there was a real poacher, it was Shot, so he was voted a very useful dog in helping to make up a bag.[1]

Of the setter breeds the Gordon was the most popular, and it was a jet-black Gordon pup purchased from Sir Alexander Cumming of Altyre that became Osgood MacKenzie's favourite dog. About the time Fan made her début Lord St John of Bletsoe had given him the winter shooting of the twenty-five islands in Loch Maree.

No ordinary dog was of any use in the islands, as one could not keep it in view for a moment among the Scots firs and birches; but with Fan all that had to be done on landing was to start her and sit comfortably on a stone or stump and wait developments. She would not be long before she came back to tell the story of her discoveries. We used to fancy we could guess by her face what kind of game she had found, and that she put on a sort of apologetic expression when it was a woodcock and not a grouse. She never wasted a moment at her point, unless we were following at her heels. She evidently argued that the only thing to be done was to find us as quickly as possible, put on a solemn face, and lead us carefully up to the game. Even black game feeding on the birch seed in the tops of the trees did not escape her, and back she would come to give us notice. She seemed to know perfectly well if birds were wild or not, and, if they were wild she would sneak along, keeping herself as low as possible, and thus giving us the tip to do likewise; but, if she felt they would be close, she would go boldly up to

40 *The Schultze process pioneered smokeless powder in the 1870s. In 1882 the more reliable E. C. powder, with cotton instead of a wood basis, superseded the original Schultze patents. An advertisement from Evan Mackenzie's* Grouse Shooting and Deer-Stalking (*1907*)

them. If we had Fan with us we never had to take a retriever. One of her wonderful talents was always appearing to know in a moment if a bird were hit or not. She would stand up on her hind-legs so as to try to mark it down as far as she could. She had another marvellous quality, which was that she could gauge whether a bird was mortally wounded or not, and she knew if she could make sure of grabbing it, or whether it would rise again and require another shot. So, if we saw Fan pointing a wounded bird and waiting for a gun to come up, then we knew it was only slightly hit; otherwise Fan managed the business herself, and spared us all trouble by stalking up to it like a cat, and then, with a sudden rush, seizing it and bringing it back to us in her mouth without the mark of a tooth on it.

The companionship and teamwork that derived from going out with a dog like Fan summed up the pleasure of this form of shooting. The way to kill the greatest number of grouse, said Charles St John, was to hunt one tract of ground thoroughly, not leaving a yard of heather untried; but to him this was far less attractive than a good stretch across a range of valley and mountain, though attended with fewer shots. He was far more pleased by seeing a brace of good dogs do their work well and exhibiting their instinct and skill, than in toiling after twice the number when hunted by a keeper, whose only plan of breaking the poor animals

41 *Picking up at the end of a drive. An engraving after Heywood Hardy from the 1890s*

was to thrash them until they were actually afraid to use half the wonderful intellect which nature had given them. 'Commend us to a plentiful sprinkling of game', wrote Christopher North, 'to ground which seems occasionally barren, and which it needs a fine instructed eye to traverse scientifically and thereof to detect the latent risks. Fear and hope are the deities of the moors, else would they lose their witchcraft. In short, we shoot like gentlemen, scholars, poets, philosophers, as we are; and looking at us you have a sight "of him who walks in glory and in joy following his dog upon the mountain-side".'[2]

Interest in the day's sport could be enlivened by a change of dogs, and where a large area of ground had to be covered and a substantial bag achieved, a team of dogs was necessary. It was customary in changing dogs to have a person meet the shooting party at an appointed time and place and to send back the dogs that had been worked to be kennelled, groomed and fed at home. By that means the new

42 *A spaniel returning the first bird in August 1924*

dogs would be quite fresh, whereas, if kept in couples following a party the whole morning, they would have been more or less on their feet from the beginning. Dogs taken from work and not sent home at once were apt to chill, stiffen and become stale and jaded. Where the shooter went out daily and stayed out all day long, three changes of dogs were not found too many to keep his kennel fresh; it was absolute ruin on young dogs in particular to keep them out too long a time.

It has always been a common custom, at least on a big range of moorland, to run a brace of dogs simultaneously. To see a good dog work is a pleasure, but to see a couple quartering the ground, each with its own territory, one to the left front of the shooting party, the other to the right, is sheer joy. When one achieves a point the other will cease its ranging and back its partner from the flank or rear. There it will remain, steady on point itself, until the first dog is moved forward and the birds flushed.

If the activities of the dog were fatiguing, that of the shooter was not necessarily so. If a sluggard he could 'ask for a little more sleep with a clear conscience, muttering as he turns himself over about the more haste and the worse speed'. To achieve a large bag, however, was obviously exhausting unless a pony was used, and in that manner the Maharaja Duleep Singh achieved the all-time record to one gun in a day over dogs of 440 birds on 12 August 1871 at Grandtully Castle. He had three brace of dogs down simultaneously and rode from point to point on a pony.

Other notable bags are 369 birds shot in one day by Colonel Campbell of Monzie in 1843 and 382 in 1846. In the 1880s Captain W. H. Tomasson killed well over 400 grouse to his own gun at Hunthill on three consecutive days, and his total of 1,200 grouse was achieved without any idea of creating a record. The hardiness of the men of that generation may be instanced by Captain Horatio Ross, who, on 12 August 1892, killed eighty-three grouse in eighty-three shots, the same being his sixty-ninth shooting season. Mr William Scott Elliot of Ankleton, Dumfriesshire, probably holds a unique record in that he died in 1901 in his ninety-first year, having been out on the moors on seventy-four successive Twelfths from 1824 to 1898.

It is a habit of grouse to get wilder as the season advances or if the weather is bad, and if shooting over dogs was to continue it was necessary to use a refined method of approaching birds. October grouse were often shot by flying a kite in front of the ranging dog, thereby simulating a bird of prey and forcing the birds to lie low. W. A. Adams described this sport as the acme of point shooting. The kite was large, much larger than the kite used over partridges in England, and was flown very high so that a large extent of ground could be covered. It was worked downwind in front of the gun, and as therefore the dog also had to work down-wind it needed to be experienced. Packs of grouse or coveys rarely sat well, but small lots and single birds generally rose within shot. They were difficult to shoot, for they went away like streaks of lightning, curling to right and left to evade the imagined bird of prey. Some people maintained that the kite harmed a moor by putting birds off the ground, but the general opinion was that if it was used in moderation, with an interval of fully ten days between each occasion, the birds returned to their territory. As an eagle will clear a beat for a day, and the birds will be back on the morrow, there is no reason to suppose that an artificial bird will do more harm. The only essential was that the shooting party maintain complete silence, for if grouse recognised the contradictory sight of men and birds of prey working in unison they would really take flight and depart.

According to Gerald Lascelles, co-author of *Coursing and Falconry*, a real hawk was as harmless to a moor as the artificial kite. His description of the picturesque and exciting sport of grouse-hawking bears reproduction in full:

> We have not infrequently, in countries where there were but few spaces open enough for hawking, flown almost daily at the same coveys, both of grouse and partridges, and found them without fail on the same feeding grounds, though in diminished numbers, as they were one by one taken; nor did flying hawks at them regularly appear to make them nearly so wild as even a day or two of shooting over the same ground. The moors where, for convenience, a separate beat is devoted to the use of hawks, it has been found that, towards the end of the season, birds lie better to dogs and are considerably more numerous than they are upon the beats where they have been shot regularly. This has been proved most conclusively upon the Achinduich moors in Sutherlandshire in 1882 and 1883, and upon the Langwell moors in Caithness in the seasons of 1885, 1886 and 1887.
>
> A good flight of game is one of the prettiest sights hawking can afford, especially when grouse is the quarry. The moor should be rather a flat one, and the less broken the ground is, the fewer burns intersect it, the better the hawk's chance of success. Grouse will 'put in' to a burn with steep sides, like a partridge into a fence, and get right underground where the banks are hollow. Good dogs are essential: they must be wide rangers, very steady, and thoroughly under-stand the sport, into which they will enter most keenly. As soon as the dog stands the falconer should unhood his hawk and throw her off. If she is an old hand at the game she will not be long mounting. Possibly, if a dashing flier, she will do so in very wide circles, ranging, it may be, a mile or more from her

master. Especially she will do this when flying hard daily, and being fully fed upon the game she is killing, she becomes full of flesh, muscle, and vitality, and at the same time what is called 'a little above herself'. Should she stray too far away the swinging of the lure, or in extreme cases, one flutter of the wing of a pigeon, will bring her back; but, as a rule, all exhibition of lures while a hawk is mounting high on the wing should be condemned. Directly she returns, and has shown by a few short turns that she is steady, the birds may be flushed. The hawk ought now to be hanging steadily, with her head to the wind, at least three gunshots high. She looks no bigger than a butterfly, and here and there bits of scud may be seen drifting between the earth and her; yet she is under command, and, should the point prove a false one, will follow her master at that lofty pitch while, say, fifty acres of heather are beaten below her. But at the right moment the falconer, who has moved quietly round so as to head his dog while the hawk gains her pitch dashes down upon the point, the birds are sprung, and the hawk, turning on her side, flies downward for a few strokes as hard as she can, and then with wings closed she falls like a stone slung from a mighty catapult, almost like a flash of light, right on to the very top of the bird she has from the first moment selected. Should she hit him fair and square, there will be a little cloud of feathers in the air, and the grouse will bound on to the heather as dead as though he had received the contents of a choke-bore at forty yards; but if the quarry pursued be an old cock grouse, perchance at the critical moment he will give three or four abrupt side shifts like those of a newly sprung snipe, and the baffled hawk will shoot up after her stoop to a height half as high as that which she came from, ready to drive at the grouse again as he scuds off to the shelter of the nearest burn. It then becomes a trial of speed between the two, the result of which depends on the distance of the flight, the lay of the ground, and similar circumstances; but the falconer will only occasionally be able to see the actual finish, and following on the line of flight will either find his falcon beneath the lee of some great boulder surrounded by a mass of feathers about to begin her feast on the body of her victim, or else hears the tinkle of her bell as the defeated hawk, having recovered her wind, takes flight again to search for her master.

It is a great advantage when the dog can be trained to dash in towards his master and flush the birds at a given signal, instead of the man having to run down and spring them himself. The dog's nose tells him exactly where the birds are. They may be at a little distance from him, and will lie like stones with the hawk overhead, so that the falconer may be unable to light upon them instantly, and the delay of a few moments may be fatal. We have seen two or

43 *Lark and Swift, the author's mother's pointers, winners of the Pointer and Setter Championships in 1960 and 1962 respectively*

three dogs of the breed of lemon and white setters, belonging to Mr St Quintin, that would dash in 'as keen as mustard' at the signal and flush the nearest grouse of the covey, dropping instantaneously as they did so. There they would remain during the time the hawk was flown, was taken up, and a fresh hawk taken from the cadge and hooded off, and after she had got to her pitch would again dash in and flush, at the exact moment, the remaining bird or birds of the covey. In this way we have seen, especially with one magnificent setter called Prince, who worked for many seasons solely with hawks, three and four flights obtained from the same point at one covey, the dog lying immovable during the long time—perhaps twenty minutes—that elapsed during the flight and taking up of the hawk in each case. Yet these dogs were no potherers, but were dashing, high ranging dogs of the highest class, thoroughly acquainted with the work they had to do, and fond of it. They were seldom used with the gun, and seemed to work with more intelligence and sense of responsibility than dogs which are shot over usually display. As a rule we have found setters more suited to hawking, and more capable of understanding the peculiar work that is required of them than pointers. This appears to have been the experience of falconers at all times, and is placed on record in various books.[3]

In recent years the practice of falconry has enjoyed a revival. The ancient esteem in which the sport is held among Arab nations, coupled with the interest which sportsmen of those nations are showing in Scottish estates, may make the flying of the peregrine against grouse a common sight again.

While falconry ranked as an aristocratic sport, the practice of netting was held in low esteem. It was associated with poaching, and indeed of the large number of grouse which were sent illicitly to English markets between August and March many were caught either with horse-hair snares set upon stooks of corn or netted. Nevertheless, if practised legitimately it was a means of culling birds which had much to recommend it. Admittedly the whole covey was caught at once, but there was no wounding and birds not required could be selected and set free. And as far as the dog was concerned, a high degree of skill was needed in remaining steady on point in the right position while the men with the net quietly drew it forward.

Of such infinite variety was the work of the pointer and setter in Victorian times. To the man who shoots grouse over dogs as to the man who hunts hound, the charm lies not so much in the killing of the quarry as in the sight of an intelligent and graceful creature in action. Each day is different, with its own problems of wind and scent and its own foibles. Physically, it can be gruelling for both dog and shooter, yet for those who are no longer agile a dog can be selected which ranges close at hand. To rest the legs or to carry the game a Highland pony can be used too, for it has been a beast of burden in the roadless Highlands from time immemorial. The obvious means of carrying deer when stalking became fashionable, it has also been an unusually docile saddle-horse for those who have wished to shoot from its back. Its origins probably stem from southern Europe, and it migrated across the land mass or over the ice about 8000 B.C. The Western Isles type of animal is smaller than that of the mainland, and the latter is often referred to as the garron. Variations in size merely reflect more or less favourable conditions of subsistence.

Sophisticated harness was developed early in the 19th century to suit the varied work the pony had to do. The mounted sportsman had a carbine bucket and strap and probably a bag on each side of the saddle behind the flaps to carry a flask and sandwich case. The docility of the beast was sometimes developed by the firing of a gun in its vicinity at feeding time. One of the most picturesque dogging scenes I have witnessed, reminiscent of former times, was an old gentleman who shot over setters from the saddle of a dun Highland mare. The latter never flinched when shots were fired. I was spared the experience which must have made a Welsh clergyman flinch who was shooting one day with Lord Anglesey. The latter, having lost a leg at Waterloo, likewise found a pony indispensable, but he succeeded in peppering the crown of the clergyman's tall hat. 'My good man, don't be afraid,' remarked his lordship, accustomed himself to remaining calm under fire, 'I'm a perfect master of the weapon.'

44 *Pointers: a detail from Richard Ansdell's* The Earl of Sefton and party returning from grouse-shooting, with a view of Glen Lyon, Perthshire, *first exhibited at the Royal Academy in 1841*

45 *Butts:* (*1*) *sunk butt;* (*2*) *cheap and nasty butt;* (*3*) *safety guards on butt;* (*4*) *double-sided butt;*
(*5*) *modern, comfortable floored, stone-built butt. An illustration by Charles Whymper from* Grouse
and Grouse Moors (*1910*) *by George Malcolm and Aymer Maxwell*

CHAPTER 8

Driving

When I hear a man say that he sees no sport in driving, I find out, in nine cases out of ten, that he is either an indifferent shot or has had little or no experience of what he is denouncing. *A. E. Gathorne-Hardy, 1899.*

Grouse-driving became an established part of the shooting scene in the north of England several decades before it became an accepted practice in Scotland. The earliest instance cannot be dated, but there were drives laid out on the Bishop of Durham's Horsley Moor by 1803, and some of the butts were in the identical position a century later. From Cannon Hall, Barnsley, near Sheffield, comes the first description of driving. When Spencer Stanhope got tired after a long day's walking after dogs, he used to sit in an old sandpit while his sons were walking Snailsden Moor nearby, and he found he got more shots than they did. Butts were put up, merely for a drive at the end of the day, but results were so good that other drives were planned. At first, three brace for a gun for a drive was considered a large bag, but as the organisation improved so did the bag, and by the early 1840s fifty brace was shot.

The new mode of shooting did not escape criticism; newspapers would announce that they were sorry to learn that the unsportsmanlike practice of driving grouse was still continued on Mr Stanhope's moors. However, participation by the aristocracy soon made it become the right thing to do, and when proprietors or tenants who enjoyed driving included Lord Ripon and the Dukes of Beaufort, Cleveland, Devonshire and Rutland, social approval was sealed.

The opponents were not all diehards. The pheasant battue was often conducted reprehensibly, and in consequence those who were acquainted only with other forms of shooting assumed that grouse-shooting was of the same pattern. The ignorant way in which covert-shooting was sometimes conducted is exemplified in the story of Colonel John Cook, inquiring of an innkeeper who had bagged the most game at a shoot; he was told that this was not known, but that the men who beat for the gentlemen killed 120 head. The beaters, evidently, had in their progress knocked on the head that number of immature pheasants. And, however well conducted the new form might be, the old sportsmen, among whom Surtees was numbered, viewed with regret the virtual disappearance of setters, pointers and spaniels. The leisurely consultation with the keeper under the gun-room window after breakfast and the informal journeying forth together was replaced by great preparation, trouble and expense. The exercise a man had in watching the working of his dogs was quite as great as sending the poor birds neck and crop over and if, as was said of coursing, you were mad for a moment and starved for an hour, so in driving you exterminated in a day what should have served you for a year. The effete young of the day, his elders asserted, was satisfied merely with an impressive set of figures in his game book; he went north without any team of dogs, even without a retriever. Ostensibly he required exercise and change of scene, but secured only the latter. He could even knock over his birds without moving from his rocking-chair, keeping iced punch and thin sandwiches within reach of his languid arm. He may dally with *The Times*, *Morning Post* or *The Field*, his head supported by an air cushion, and kill his right and left with the most cool indifference. Meanwhile he can signal to his observant man that he requires fresh refections.

Such contemptuous condemnation of driving did not last long and did not have much effect, but in Scotland driving was slow in coming to the fore and for this there were several reasons. One was the fact that in remote areas the idea of killing large bags was quite properly out of place, because difficulties of communication made disposal impossible. At Gairloch, for example, game was shot for the house or to give to estate tenants, and there were neither steamers nor railways nor even wheeled transport to convey it elsewhere. Even if surplus game could be effectively disposed of, the assembling of beaters could not be done on a lonely moor. At Auchnafree in Perthshire Colonel Whitaker overcame this problem by building a small barrack with ten rooms and a mess-room. He engaged beaters by the month and was rewarded by seeing bags climb from under a thousand to 6,000 brace.

Keepers were resistant to change, for their own reasons. The Highland gamekeeper was by instinct a hunter and his job was to furnish game for his master's table. He disliked and despised labouring, and so he looked askance at the idea of building butts and digging drains. Even the destruction of vermin was not recognised as being of much importance, and heather burning was carried out only where sheep grazing prevailed. On shooting grounds heather was left tall under the mistaken idea that it was best left tall where grouse were more important than sheep. Furthermore, keepers made some useful income from training and selling dogs, and in the innovation of driving they thought they foresaw a perquisite about to disappear. For this they could not be blamed; their job was not well paid at the best of times, and often a shooting tenant, having paid a rent out of proportion to the value of his moor, became stingy on matters of wages and was rewarded with poor sport in consequence.

That the driving of grouse did become the commonest form of shooting was due as much as anything else to an inevitable chain of circumstances. Increased demand for shooting led to better moor management, scientific heather burning and wholesale destruction of vermin, with grouse moors in consequence becoming overstocked. Driving was the obvious method of shooting late in the season when birds would not sit to dogs and large numbers had still to be killed to avoid disease. It was realised also that a moor which is occasionally driven suffers far less from disturbance than one which is shot continuously over dogs.

The killing of large bags was facilitated by the introduction of smokeless powder in the 1870s. Hitherto, rapid fire was inhibited by the fact that the discharge of a first barrel loaded with the old black powder on a damp and windless day produced a cloud of smoke. The shooter's view was obscured to such an extent that he had to change ground before he could fire his second barrel. There was no such problem with the new powder, which was manufactured initially from nitrated wood sawdust on the basis of the Schultze patents. In 1882 the more reliable E.C. powder was introduced, with cotton instead of a wood basis, although smokeless powder did not come into general use until a few years later. The delay was due not so much to defects in the powder as to defects in the loading: country gunmakers all loaded by measure in place of by weight and to produce an even batch of smokeless cartridges loading by weight was essential.

The popularity of driven grouse was enhanced by royal patronage. King Edward VII's varied sporting interests dictated that after his customary visit to a continental spa and his attendance at Cowes and Doncaster Races he had little time left for residence at Balmoral. His stay there was of necessity late in the season as a rule, when birds were too wild to sit to dogs. In his younger days as Prince of Wales he did rent ground from Farquharson of Invercauld for shooting over pointers and setters, though stalking was probably his first love. In later years, when he was not fit for much physical exertion, he rented South Gairnside and Micras Moor from Invercauld for driving. He would also spend some time shooting with his friends, notably Lord Burton at Glenquoich and Arthur Sassoon at Tulchan Lodge, where the grouse were particularly good. Tulchan was a favourite base, for from there he could visit Cawdor, Cullen, Gordon Castle and Castle Grant.

46 *The Prince of Wales (afterwards King George V) riding to the butts in the early 1900s*

The art of driving grouse, which anyone who has practised it will agree is the study of a lifetime, was developed ponderously. At first it was believed that hilly ground could not be driven, whereas in fact grouse will follow the contours of the hills and can thus be induced to fly to the desired spot more readily on uneven ground. Early driving was sometimes conducted without butts, but faced with an expanse of open moor the shooter tends to be visible over a mile of heather and grouse will avoid any semblance of a human being on their course. Abel Chapman wrote in the 1920s:

> It would certainly surprise anyone accustomed to grouse driving on the regular lines to find how immensely the difficulties are increased by the absence of butts. As a rule the grouse-shooter walks straight into his commodious station skilfully situated half-hidden under the hill, yet in a dominating position where, himself unseen, he commands a clear view both ahead and all around. He leaves his gun in a convenient corner, lays out a few cartridges ready, and hangs up his spy-glass what time his eye is registering all the salient points of his field-of-action.[1]

There is no fear that the grouse will shy away because for twelve months they have flown past the butt and they are not likely to notice a head peering over on this particular morning.

In the 19th century butts were often known as batteries, an expansive term which reflected the fact that they were built to contain three men and a dog. The line would contain only three or four batteries, but the shooter might have been using three guns and would therefore need room for two loaders as well as himself. Few sportsmen nowadays shoot with three guns, and fewer can boast of taking five birds out of a covey. This was done by killing the first bird far out in front with the choke barrel, changing guns and getting a right and left again in front and finally, with the third gun, getting a right and left behind.

47 *The Prince of Wales (afterwards King George V) in the butts, c. 1906. Note the two cartridges in the loader's fingers for speed of reloading*

The construction and shape of the butt has changed little over the years. Ideally, it is partially dug out or sunk, with the parapet built up of turf, or of stones lined over with turf. Butts that are totally sunk, i.e. dug out so that the shooter is in a sort of wide trench, are usually susceptible to flooding or to the sides falling in. In any event the floor of a butt should be covered with some material to prevent one sinking into the peat, which is not only uncomfortable for the feet but also renders it quite impossible to swing the gun. Flat stones make an ideal floor, and in the absence of stones duckboards can be laid down though they are apt to be slippery. Whatever the base, a layer of turf on the floor stops feet slipping, and a drain led to the outside runs off excess water.

A good butt in a well-placed line is a joy to the eye and a comfort to be within. An ill-conceived line of butts is horrible to look at and diverts birds from their intended line of flight. Butts made of wood are admissible where experiments are being done to find out where a permanent line is best situated, but corrugated iron is excruciating. Building should never be done on a skyline, but if possible the line should be 50 yards or more back from the crest of a reverse slope so that there is adequate vision in front and at the same time the birds do not shy away from anything unusual visible in the butts. Wherever the line is, in the interests of safety it must be a straight one. This means that for one butt the field of view may be wide while the next has a short skyline, but this is inevitable. Where, because of ground contours, one butt is invisible to another a post should be put in the ground visible to each as a reminder. Often, but not always, it is possible to make one line of butts serve drives from each direction, but where the contours of the ground render it necessary a second line should be built for the return drive. It is wise to construct more butts than there are guns to fill them, that is ten or eleven butts for the customary seven to nine guns, for on different days it will be prudent to place the guns to suit the currently prevailing wind direction.

> Sir Norman had lived all his life in accordance with King's Regulations, or Field Service Regulations, or the veteran wisdom of the Badminton Library, and never yet had these or the birds let him down. His moors had, with due allowance for the wind and the occasional shift of butts uphill or down, been driven more or less in the same way for seventeen years, Banchovie one day, Glencairn the next. It was the old way, the accepted way, the custom of his predecessors, the tradition of the moor. No birds had ever dared to flout that solemn ritual . . . To change beats in the middle of a day's grouse-driving was almost like playing the Eton and Harrow match in September. (J. K. Stanford, *The Twelfth*, p. 71.)

48 *Lord Woolavington shooting during a house-party at Mannock Moors, August 1922. Before his elevation to the peerage, James Buchanan (1849–1935) was a distiller and later became a noted racehorse owner and philanthropist*

The pioneer of driving in Scotland was The MacKintosh of Moy in Inverness-shire. Apart from assiduous attention to proper burning and the destruction of vermin he evolved the principle of placing the butts so that they should be as inconspicuous as possible and set in the carefully observed line of flight of birds. An interesting aspect of Moy methods was that butts were placed not more than 15 yards apart at some drives. It was found that neighbouring guns, paradoxically, did not shoot each other's birds and were less likely to shoot each other than when they were far apart. Nor did the bag of birds suffer on account of the shortness of the line, for driving was conducted on the principle that rather than covering as long a line as possible the flight of birds should be concentrated into the smallest space in order that all the guns could have shots at the concentrated birds. All this was in contrast to generally accepted practice for the butts were customarily 80 to 100 yards apart. Such wide spacing (45 or 50 yards is normal spacing today) was dictated erroneously more by consideration of the danger of guns wounding each other than by consideration of birds being wounded at extreme range. Accidents, such as the Duke of Roxburghe being shot in the face by Lord Chesterfield at 180 yards, the force of the shot being such that the blood ran down the wounded man's shirt, were cited to prove the point. To obviate further the danger of blue blood being shed so effusively, it was recommended that screens should be placed between each butt. In fact, reasonably close placing of butts makes for greater safety because the guns are more conspicuous to each other and each man is more aware of the exact position of his neighbour.

The person in command of a grouse drive, namely the keeper, has a skilled job to perform. Not only must he control his line of beaters and ensure that they are properly spaced, but he must also ensure that his line marches directly on to the line of butts. On a misty day it can be a very difficult task. Lastly, he has to provide flankers who know their job. Two or three of the latter are spaced out, probably 50 to 100 yards from each other, at each end of the line of guns and about forty-five degrees from that line. Their purpose is to turn birds towards the guns if they are inclining to break out at the sides. That sounds easier than it is, for if the flanker stands up and waves his flag when the birds are more than about 75 yards away they will either fly back over the beaters or be even more resolute to break away at the sides. The expert flanker will lie concealed in the heather until the birds are about 50 yards away and will then reveal himself so that their angle of flight is just so deflected that they are coaxed over the butts. Split-second timing is necessary, and nothing is so frustrating as the sight of an over-enthusiastic but ignorant flanker doing more harm than good by turning birds back that might otherwise have come in range of the guns. The good flanker is not easy to find nowadays.

Grouse-driving is the most dangerous of all forms of shooting in Britain. The attributes of the sport lend themselves to this—a fast and often low approach of birds and the tendency for butts to be at different altitudes owing to the contours of the ground. To aim at a high bird may be to aim at butts further up the hillside, and it is very easy to swing on a low bird and, before one realises it, continue the swing through the line of butts. In this manner my mother and my uncle were quite seriously injured in two separate butts by a gun in a third butt, some years ago. It is wise to place two vertical sticks on the left and right front of the butt to restrict the arc of fire. The sticks should be of sufficient length to prevent the shooter bobbing his gun over them! Only rarely can the victim of a shooting accident benefit, but such was the fortune of Sir John Astley[2] when shooting with the Duke of Rutland at Longshaw. Having been warned that a certain William Morris was a trifle dangerous, Astley was apprehensive when in drawing lots for places he found himself next to him. All went well on the first day till after lunch when, as the butts were somewhat close, Astley bid his loader build up the side of his hiding-place as a precaution. Presently a large pack of grouse came sailing over; he let go two shots in front, snatched up the second gun to have another two shots as they passed him and swinging round took a pace to the rear and got out of his hide. Prompt advantage was taken by Wicked Bill (Morris's nickname), who put a couple of pellets into Astley's right cheek and, in the latter's own words, nailed him just as if he was a buck rabbit popping his head out of a hole. However he was none the worse; in fact, all the better, for he was asked to Morris's first-rate shooting in Norfolk as an honourable amendment.

As the guns came out of the lodge half an hour later to the waiting motor-cars, Sir Norman held out a little sheaf of numbered cards and each of his guests drew one. The cards bore the superscription 'Banchovie Lodge, Aberdeenshire', and beneath in Sir Norman's neat handwriting the date, the beat, and the names of the guns in due order of social precedence. There was a space for the total bag and one for the gun's 'claim' for each drive. By this means at the end of the day Sir Norman could reckon up the bag against his guests' claims and have a useful cross-check against any purloining of game by beaters. (J. K. Stanford, *The Twelfth*, pp. 65–6.)

In all matters of shooting a code of honour exists today as it did then, but there was extended to the older generation a deference which would be considered

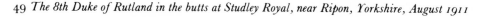

49 *The 8th Duke of Rutland in the butts at Studley Royal, near Ripon, Yorkshire, August 1911*

50 Not to be Turned *by Thorburn. The flag is waved to deflect birds over the guns, but here in vain*

unnecessary by modern standards. A young man was not supposed to be an unerring shot nor expected to tell good stories, and if his elder neighbour missed a bird with both barrels it was tactful to let the bird go rather than wipe his eye. The practice of conferring congratulations on those who brought down difficult birds was also deemed bad practice. Such deference to the aged or infirm was in itself conducive to the acceptance of driving, for not only was it hard on an old man to toil up a hillside to a dog on point, perhaps with birds running in front; it was hard too on the dog when the gun was not within range of the birds when they rose.

The controversy between the votaries of driving and shooting over dogs died a natural death; each form of shooting was and is accorded a place in sport. There is nothing more beautiful than to see a pair of well-trained pointers or setters ranging a moor, and nothing more impressive than the sight of a first-class shot crumple up his birds. The bird rising from the spot marked by a point cannot compare. Perhaps the ideal moor is where the birds sit well to dogs early in the season and the drivers get their turn later on. As for the softness of the sedentary shooter, there can be nothing colder than waiting in a butt for October grouse. A Member of Parliament was once guilty of the heinous crime of lighting a fire in his butt and going to sleep, letting the grouse stream over his head uninjured.

If the skill necessary to shoot driven grouse was not denied by anyone, excuses for poor form always have been numerous. Augustus Grimble listed forty, all of which he claimed had been heard in mitigation of bad workmanship:

1 Dust in my eyes.
2 Sun in my eyes.
3 Wind in my eyes.
4 They swerved as I pulled.
5 Could not see them till they were on me.
6 Never saw them till they were past me.
7 The light is so horridly bright.
8 Such a beastly dull light.
9 The box was too high.
10 The boxes are not half high enough.
11 A new gun.
12 Cartridges damp.
13 Had a letter from my wife this morning.
14 Cartridges too heavily loaded.
15 So cold I could not swing to them.

51 Why Turn Round? *by Thorburn. There are still plenty to shoot in front*

16 Never can shoot well if forced to sit in a box.

17 Caught a chill yesterday.

18 Bilious this morning.

19 Took two pills last night.

20 All the fault of that glass of port after champagne.

21 It's drinking that silly lemon squash.

22 Fingers so cold could not feel the triggers.

23 Rheumatics in my elbow.

24 A lady in the butt.

25 The loader got in the way.

26 Birds out of shot.

27 Pipe on the wrong side of my mouth.

28 'Bacca smoke in my eyes.

29 The driving seat broke.

30 Too many cigars last night.

31 The whiskey of old Smith's is not good.

32 The cook gave notice this morning.

33 Flo refused me yesterday.

34 Boots too tight.

35 Coat cuts my arms.

36 Never can shoot when Smith is next to me.

37 Got a dunning letter this morning.

38 Been threatened with an action of breach of promise.

39 The eggs were hard boiled at breakfast.

40 Lost every rubber last night.[3]

In the books of records Scotland holds only a modest place compared to England, for the northern English moors have always yielded larger bags. The record was attained on 12 August 1915, on the Littledale and Abbeystead moors of 12,000 acres in Lancashire, when 2,929 grouse were shot in six drives. The individual record is held by Lord Walsingham at Blubberhouse in Northumberland. In 1872, that vintage year which saw greater bags of grouse than ever before or since, he shot 842 grouse in sixteen drives throughout a day of rather over twelve hours. He beat his own record in 1888 by killing 1,070 grouse in twenty drives during a period of fourteen hours.

Lord Walsingham's feat was consciously attempted, which makes the more remarkable Sir Frederick Milbank's achievement in 1872 of killing at Wemmergill in Yorkshire 730 birds out of a total of 2,070 in a day's driving. He

ONE OF THE ADVANTAGES OF SHOOTING
FROM A BUTT

Keeper (on moor rented by the latest South African millionaire, to guest). " Never mind the birds, sir. For onny sake, lie down! The maister's gawn tae shoot!"

was merely a member of a team of guns and no efforts were made to direct the birds particularly over him. In one drive he killed 190 grouse in twenty-three minutes. Only twice during the day did he kill two birds in one shot, but they came in such a constant stream that not for one second did he stop shooting, except to allow his loaders to finish loading. During the whole season he killed 18,231 grouse.

The moors of Scotland attract more by their setting and by the test of skill that driven birds give than from record-breaking capacity. The Buccleuch estates on the borders of Dumfriesshire and Roxburghshire have always been particularly productive, and there on eight recorded days between 1911 and 1915 bags averaged 733 brace a day. In the north, 1872 saw a total of 7,000 birds killed in the season on Dalnadamph and 10,600 at Glenbucket over dogs.

A notable point about these Victorian shooting statistics is the handicap the performers imposed upon themselves by the clothes they wore. Heavy shooting coats and waistcoats and stiff white collars must have made it a tiring business, and for the loaders it was no less exhausting humping round and manipulating bagfuls of solid brass cartridges.

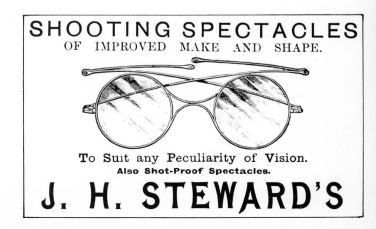

SHOOTING SPECTACLES
OF IMPROVED MAKE AND SHAPE.

To Suit any Peculiarity of Vision.
Also Shot-Proof Spectacles.

J. H. STEWARD'S

53 *An advertisement from* Something About Guns and Shooting (*1891 edn.*) *by 'Purple Heather'*

It was clear from the moment they took their places that the moor was alive with birds: one great lot rose with a roar off the ridge which masked the butts and went back into the drive; and a host of birds in ones and twos kept rising and following them. From where he was in the top butt, the General could see a little ridge a mile and a half away, and over and along it streamed from minute to minute scores of little black dots, like midges, which meant grouse coming into the centre of the beat.

'By Gad, Tom!' he exclaimed to his loader. 'Old Tye was right! I never saw so many grouse. Have we got enough cartridges, do you think?'

'I've got 120 here, sir,' said Tom, 'and we can get at the other bag before the next drive. They should do us!'

The guns waited in tense silence, eyes roving along the ridge, safety-catches forward, each loader stooping behind them with the second gun and two more cartridges held in the knuckles of the right hand. Here was the team in action, knowing exactly what to do. (J. K. Stanford, *The Twelfth*, pp. 73–4.)

HOPE.

DOUBT

DESPAIR.

DISGUST.

G D ARMOUR

54 '*Old Dogs and New Masters*' *from G. D. Armour's* Sport 'and there's the humour of it'

55 *The end of a grouse-drive: beaters with flags approach butts*

The excitement of grouse-driving does not lend itself as readily to purple prose passages as the slower but more gracious dogging. Lord Granville Gordon, however, captured the essential difficulty of the sport when he described the approaching bird as

almost invisible, with a strong wind behind him, and quick indeed must be the hand and eye that comes into quick play to drop the passing bird bouncing on the heather. The singletons are the easiest bagged. The confusion is when a pack rises on the far sky-line, then vanishes for some moments in the purple gloom, while there comes borne on the breeze the faint 'Mark over!' of the approaching beaters. See! the birds are coming straight for you: a hundred thousand forms seem to float in the air with motionless wings. You pick out one which seems first; no, there are others before him. You change your mind and your bird. Bang! . . . missed him. Bang! . . . missed again.

'Quick, Henry, the other gun.' Revenge! you will brown the lot . . . bang! bang! not a feather is ruffled, and the whole pack skims away to the glen behind. Through your mind there goes a quick resolve to give your guns to your man and bid him throw them in the loch![4]

For the most picturesque description of grouse-driving that I know of we must turn to 'The Last Drive', one of Patrick Chalmers's poems. I select three verses:

> The gales are gotten up with night,
> The stormy West's a-hum,
> And hardly there'll be shooting light
> To last till beaters come;
> I hear a grouse-cock's wild GO BACK,
> I see a kindling star
> Redden amid the flying wrack
> Above the braes of Mar.
>
> But look, a lot's aloft and on;
> A whistle bids us mark;
> Cowards, curling from the butts they're gone
> Across the wind and dark;
> Again, again—*these* shall not shirk,
> They're here a headlong cloud,
> And crackling through the gusty mirk,
> The batteries bark aloud.
>
> Like thunderbolt of Jove, amain
> Hurls through the darkling sky;
> Hold yards ahead, and *yards* ahead,
> And breathe a prayer to Pan . . .
> He crumples and he crashes, dead
> As Caesar or Queen Anne.[5]

PART FOUR

The Season

The yacht lying off a coastal moor gave variety to holiday pleasures. This particular yacht, The Netta, *was photographed in Loch Leven in 1899*

CHAPTER 9

August

If you could throw a net over the Highlands in August, you would catch nine-tenths of the genius and glory of Great Britain. *The 'Idstone' Papers, 1872*

By the 1870s Scotland in autumn had become a social event which, like all social events centred on sport, attracted not only those who were participants but leading members of society as well. In 1822 Lady Francis Leveson-Gower had complained of the dullness of Dunrobin Castle, seat of the Dukes of Sutherland: '. . . not a book or a piece of work to be seen, the company formed into a circle and every man and his wife sitting next to each other'. Fifty years later she would have been dull herself had she so complained; at Dunrobin, as at the other great houses of Scotland the figures of history flitted across the stage. The Queen and Stanley the explorer stayed. Sir Ronald Gower, travelling there by rail, found himself in a carriage with John Bright, the latter on his way to fish at Boat o' Garten but so eager to talk of his meeting with Gladstone and his failure to change the Prime Minister's mind on the Irish Question that he missed his station and went on to Grantown. A few years later Lord Rosebery, then Prime Minister, was at the Castle, praising the view from the terrace as the most beautiful he had ever seen and playing with the Sutherland children, attracted to him by the fuss he made of them. Between times he killed four stags in the forest and was probably the first Prime Minister to do so.

From Glamis we have a delightful vignette of the talent for self-entertainment. The seven sons and three daughters of the Earl of Strathmore were born musicians. They were always singing, whether they were on their way to a cricket match, on the road home from shooting, in the middle of dinner, they could not help bursting into harmony. In the oak-panelled dining-room, its great Jacobean chimneypiece rising to the roof, it was the custom after dinner for the two family pipers to make the circuit of the table three times, and then to walk slowly off, still playing, through the old stone passages until the last faint echoes of the music had died away. Then all the lights in the dining-room were extinguished except the candles on the table, out came a tuning fork, and one note was sounded. 'Madrigal from *Ruddigore*, "Spring is Come", third beat,' said the conducting brother, and off they went, singing exquisitely, glees, madrigals, part-songs, anything and everything, the acoustic properties of the lofty room adding to the effect. When Gladstone visited Glamis in 1884 he asked for a part-song in the middle of dinner, and as the singing was continued in the drawing-room afterwards, he asked whether the young people would allow an old man to sing bass in the glees with them. He went away next day saying that he had not enjoyed himself so much for many months.

Whatever outsiders may have thought or said about society pleasures, to many of the Highland people the sportsmen were always welcome invaders. They gave regular employment of a nature which suited the Highland temperament, and which could be combined with crofting as a secondary employment. Summer and autumn visitors were the mainstay of places along the railway lines, and owners or tenants of mansions and shooting-lodges forfeited local popularity only when they got their goods from the Army and Navy or other London stores.

The benefits that accrued to the Highlanders derived from an expensive amusement, once the autumn holiday became an event in the social calendar. Proceeds of sale of game could go some way to defraying a modest sportsman's expenses if he lived quietly off his land, but for those who visited Scotland on holiday and engaged the inevitable retinue it was never a cheap pastime. A rental of £1 a brace, to include lodge and keeper but not gillies or ponies, was a fair rent about 1870, but by the end of the century a good moor might have fetched twice that sum. In addition, gillies usually got £1 a week, feeding and lodging themselves, but they expected lunch and whisky when they went to the hill. Beaters were paid 2s a day and lunch if men, and boys got a shilling. Hire of a pony to carry the game panniers was £1 a week. Respectable pointers and setters could be purchased for between £10 and £35 each and a good working retriever was £10, rising to £100 for an outstanding animal.

The guest had no worries over these overheads, but if he wished to cut a bit of a dash on his holiday he could incur considerable outlay. On top of every sportsman's basic expenses of game licence at £3, gun licence 10s and cartridges 10s a hundred, a best London handmade gun cost from £60 to £90 and the Birmingham equivalent from £45 to £50. Good machine-made guns were 17 guineas or less. One would applaud the purchase of a tweed shooting-suit at perhaps 6 guineas, for it is a curious fact that then, as now '. . . your country gentleman who gets himself up in the latest fashion, and will shoot with a pair of hammerless ejectors that cost him £160, may often be seen using them when clad

57 *The Prince of Wales (afterwards King Edward VII) and others at Derry Lodge, Mar Forest, Aberdeenshire*

in a morning coat in which he would scarcely venture an appearance at the village fair'. Last, but not least, tips to the keeper were high in relation to the accepted sum today. For a first-class day's driving £1 was normal, and 5s was the minimum for a modest day's shooting.

The custom of the rich to have a steam yacht lying off their coastal moors was a costly one. A vessel suitable for making trips during the day and returning to shore at night would have a displacement of up to 60 tons and cost about £4,000. Crew would number four or five and total expenses would be £15 a week to keep the yacht in commission. The larger sea-going yacht could often be purchased for a modest sum in relation to its size because so few people could afford them. It might weigh up to 200 tons, cost up to £10,000, and have accommodation for the owner and four or five friends.

All this is a far cry from the days when sport could be had for the asking, or at

58 *Alfresco lunch in the Highlands: The Prince of Wales (seated, centre) and others in 1872*

least huge tracts of moorland could be rented for £25 or so. It was still possible, as now, to have some cheap sport, live in a bothy and equip oneself with tinned food, but in respect of costly sport it is only fair to admit that the demands of tenants as regards accommodation, furniture and sanitary arrangements had greatly increased and that a very large proportion of the apparent increase of rent represented interest on outlay necessitated by such demands. Criticism can be levelled at the extravagant living, so alien and distasteful to an earlier, more spartan generation, but sport retained its wild character and the sportsman who brought home his grouse or his stag had, in most instances, earned the badge of the hunter. For some who tasted the fashion for Scottish sport the result was a second home in the Highlands which came to be handed down from generation to generation, while for others once was enough. In the latter class one Englishman wrote with good humour to a friend that he was

> more than thankful . . . that my lease of Benmackwhappie's deer forest and grouse moors has at length come to a close. I have had the confounded place now for three seasons, and it has cost me in that time not less than £10,000 all told, in addition to no end of small sums of which I grew tired of keeping a note. Believe me, I have never before worked so hard—not even when I wore the

clogs in my father's dye shop—as I have done at deer-stalking. Had I time to narrate all my experiences, comic and serious, you would get many a hearty laugh out of them. For a couple of hours at a time I have walked with water of a running stream well over my boots. A suit of clothes has been done for in a day's time, twice or thrice I have sunk up to my chest in a moss, once I fell over a precipice and startled a herd of deer, much to the disgust of my forester, Allister Mackenzie, whom no quantity of whisky would pacify. He sulked over the event during the remainder of the day, and doubtless he thought my hurts were well deserved and not severe enough for the sin I had committed. On one occasion whilst out fishing on Loch Whappie, I fell overboard, and was not fished up till I was nearly drowned. On another occasion, when I was creeping about in a plantation of young larches, I was fired at by one of my own gillies, who said he mistook me for a beastie, of what kind I know not, but I fancy I had a rather narrow escape. Per contra, I have on five occasions brought down a good stag, at an extra cost all round for my baptism. So much for my career as a deer-stalker in the Highlands of Scotland.

59 *The bag after a successful day, Studley Royal, near Ripon, Yorkshire, August 1911*

60 *After a day on the moors — Empire songs under empyreal skies. An advertisement from Hall's directory,* Highland Sportsman

The Scottish season had a serious side to it too. It gave opportunity in a relaxed atmosphere and environment for people from the different professions and political parties that made up the nation's leaders to come together informally and thresh out current problems. House parties were not necessarily composed of men of similar political views and differences of opinion could be settled or harmonised away from the debating chamber in the more civilised and soothing surroundings of a place like Dunrobin. In the farflung outposts a galaxy of talent gathered in the autumn; while Lord Rosebery was staying with the Sutherlands in 1894 Mr Stead, Editor of *The Times,* was also a guest, as was Miss Shaw, correspondent on colonial matters for that newspaper, while down at the manse at Golspie Mr Nicholson, Librarian of the Bodleian, was writing a book on Golspie and its folk-lore.

Inevitably there was a snobbish aspect, which was ridiculed by Anthony Trollope in *The Eustace Diamonds:*

A great many people go to Scotland in the autumn. When you have your autumn holiday in hand to dispose of it, there is nothing more aristocratic that you can do than go to Scotland. Dukes are more plentiful there than in Pall Mall, and you will meet an earl or at least a lord on every mountain. Of course, if you merely travel about from inn to inn, and neither have a moor of your own nor stay with any great friend, you don't quite enjoy the cream of it; but to go to

61 *Beaters, keepers and dogs enjoy a working lunch on the moor*

62 *Collecting up grouse at the Earl of Ancaster's shoot at Drummond Castle, near Crieff, September 1922. This estate adjoins the author's own moor*

Scotland in August, and stay there, perhaps, till the end of September, is about the most certain step you can take towards autumnal fashion. Switzerland and the Tyrol, and even Italy are all redolent of Mr Cook and in those beautiful lands, you become subject at least to suspicion.

By no persons was the duty of adhering to the best side of society more clearly appreciated than by Mr and Mrs Hittaway of Warwick Square. . . . The names of Mr and Mrs Hittaway were constantly in the papers. They were invited to evening gatherings at the houses of both alternate Prime Ministers. They were to be seen at fashionable gatherings up the river. They attended concerts at Buckingham Palace. Once a year they gave a dinner-party which was inserted in *The Morning Post*. On such occasions at least one Cabinet

Minister always graced the board. In fact, Mr Hittaway, as Chairman of the Board of Civil Appeals, was somebody; and Mrs Hittaway, as his wife and as sister to a peer, was somebody also.

There is this drawback upon the happy condition which Mr Hittaway had achieved—that it demands a certain expenditure. . . . It therefore resulted that when Mr and Mrs Hittaway went to Scotland, which they would endeavour to do every year, it was very important that they should accomplish their aristocratic holiday as visitors at the house of some aristocratic friend. So well had they played their cards in this respect, that they seldom failed altogether. In one year they had been the guests of a great marquis quite in the north, and that had been a very glorious year. To talk of Stackallan was, indeed, a thing of beauty. But in that year Mr Hittaway had made himself very useful in London. Since that they had been at delicious shooting lodges in Ross and Inverness-shire, had visited a millionaire at his palace amidst the Argyle mountains, had been feted in a western island, had been bored by a Dundee dowager, and put up with a Lothian laird. But the thing had been almost always done, and the Hittaways were known as people that went to Scotland. He could handle a gun, and was clever enough never to shoot a keeper. She could read aloud, could act a little, could talk and hold her tongue; and let her hosts be who they would and as mighty as you please, never caused them trouble by seeming to be out of their circle, and on that account requiring peculiar attention.[1]

While shooters shot and social climbers tried to seep through, the ladies were broadening the scope of their occupations. The sportsman who visited Scotland early in Queen Victoria's reign and was still doing so in the 1880s could reflect, probably with some regrets, on the great changes in the nature of his holiday. High rents replaced almost-free sport, railways had ended the quiet but glorious era of the stage-coach and lastly, by the closing decades of the century, women had gained a firm foothold on the hill.

63 *Alfresco lunch near Balmoral, 1933. From right, anticlockwise: The Duke of York (later King George VI), Sir Frederick Ponsonby, Neville Wigram, The Hon. Alexander Hardinge, Sir Derek Keppel, Major Levidis, and King George II of the Hellenes*

CHAPTER 10

Ladies!

The ladies thought they would go out shooting: countenance of the gentlemen on beholding them (*Cromlix game book*)

The idea that the ladies should go to Scotland at all, far less beyond the drawing room, the lawns and the gravelled paths, was received with mixed feelings by the men. Augustus Grimble asserted that bachelor parties were more apt to run smoothly than those of married men, for if four Benedicts brought their respective wives to an out-of-the-way shooting-box, and the ladies were young and good-looking, the chances were great that one of the men would soon be paying more attention to the wife of one of his friends than to his own lawful spouse.

A more heinous crime, to those who regarded their grouse-shooting as a serious matter, was the distraction the fair sex caused; Mr Reginald Dobbes, in Trollope's *The Duke's Children*, said there should be no women in Scotland—just an old one here and there, who would know how to cook grouse. He was not pleased, therefore, when Lord Silverbridge declared his intention of going over one morning to the neighbouring estate of Killancodlem, where Mabel Grex was staying.

'A lot of men and women who pretend to come there for shooting,' said Dobbes angrily, 'but do all the mischief they can.'
'One must go and see one's friends, you know.'
'Some girl!' said Dobbes.

One must sympathise with Dobbes, for the experiences of one writer of the period will have been shared on occasion by most shooting men.

Ladies are very fond of putting in an appearance at a shooting lunch; this is all very well if they go home with the empty dishes, but when you are addressed as follows in a pleading tone; 'Oh! Mr So-and-so, *do* you mind me standing beside you while you shoot?' What are you to do unless you are downright rude and

4 *Detail from* The Earl of Sefton and party returning from grouse-shooting,
ith a view of Glen Lyon, Perthshire *by Richard Ansdell, R.A.*

Ladies! · 131

refuse point blank; your sport is spoilt for the afternoon if you are one of the guns posted forward, in covert shooting especially. Ladies will not and cannot keep quiet, they get excited and make the birds break back. I cannot vote for woman suffrage in the shooting field.

A particular incident when a woman would have been judged unwelcome by any criterion, was described by Grimble in *Highland Sport*, and is reminiscent of a cartoon by H. M. Bateman; the party was assembling at the lodge at the beginning of their tenancy:

> Captain Spiller was to arrive in time for dinner, but as he was late, after giving him fair law, we sat down without him, and hardly done so before the wheels of his conveyance were heard outside, and in a few minutes the Captain entered, when with a bow to us and a shake of the Colonel's hand he rattled out a torrent of speech more rapidly and jerkily spoken than anything I had ever heard before.
>
> 'Here *we* are, Colonel,' exclaimed he; 'Make you stare, I know, to hear me say *we*, but I've brought my wife! Only married five days, you know; couldn't leave her behind me, could I? Didn't even think of getting spliced when I settled with you; the whole thing done in a jiffey. So now I'll just run up and change, and we will be down in no time!' And before the Colonel had recovered from the news of Mrs Spiller, the Captain was off.[1]

The bride and bridegroom turned out to be a singularly unattractive couple, and the Colonel could not be blamed for his resentment, but the building of comfortable shooting-lodges and greater ease of travel made parties *en famille* a matter of course.

The diehards might have deplored mixed parties, but for the young it was fun. Fathers would take a moor with an eye to their daughters, for whom were selected young men who in their turn might find more scope for their initiative by going north to do their wooing and taking a suitable place. In the latter category was Harry, who 'during last London season became enamoured of a very pretty and accomplished girl'.

> He had some reason to believe that his admiration and devotion were not unfavourably regarded by the object of his affections. He soon learned, though, that his attentions were unmistakably unpalatable to her people, who had higher matrimonial ideas for their only daughter. Though a bright, handsome fellow, well-educated and with considerable fortune, Harry, unfortunately for

65 *Turmoil on the moors: women and midges (Cromlix game book)*

himself, in their eyes, had a father, now deceased, who in his time had been a very well-known manufacturer. He had been, in fact, a self-made man, able to give his son the education and upbringing of a gentleman and leave him a tidy fortune—that was all.

The Vavasours, on the other hand, . . . could boast of a long line of more or less illustrious ancestors, and though these ancestors had left them very little money and a heavily encumbered estate, they conferred upon them an undeniable claim to position in the bluest of blue-blooded circles. The course of true love never did run smooth, and it was, I fancy, running pretty roughly with

66 *Sketch of a gillie assisting a 'new woman' (from* Mr Punch in the Highlands), *probably by J. Priestman Atkinson, who worked for* Punch *from 1865 to 1893*

MISS LAVINIA BROUNJONES'S ADVENTURES
IN THE HIGHLANDS
Lavinia takes a siesta,

And the frightful situation she finds herself in at the end
of it.

Harry towards the end of last season in town, when he learned that Miss Vavasour and her brother were going to the Highlands for August and September, on a visit to some distant relatives who had taken a shooting-box there.

Young Harry, discovering that the shooting adjoining the Vavasours was to be let, took it for the season. His object was not so much to place himself on a Scottish grouse moor for the first time in his life as to situate himself within calling distance of the lovely Miss Vavasour. He installed an aunt in charge of his shooting-lodge, and there was much exchange of hospitality between the neighbours.

The state of affairs between Harry and his lady love was brought to a climax when Miss Vavasour, who was fond of driving a pair of spirited ponies in a basket carriage, lost control of them on a steep and narrow road. Harry, who was shooting nearby, saw the phaeton coming down the hill at ever-increasing speed and ran to assist. He seized the ponies, threw his weight against them and, with the aid of the keeper, brought them to a standstill. The injuries he sustained, though minor, were such that the Vavasours insisted he could not return home for a few days. Miss Vavasour, of course, proved to be the best of nurses.

When Harry left, only parental blessing was needed before the engagement was announced. Old Mr Vavasour came north at his daughter's earnest request; he could hold out no longer, and settlements were satisfactorily worked out.

Cupid's bow was not the only weapon that induced ladies to the north. Some were content merely to accompany the luncheon basket, while others wielded rod and gun. They were surprised and encouraged by the liberal attitude which Scotsmen bore towards women. The great ladies of Edinburgh enjoyed a prestige comparable to the ladies of the French salons. They were not necessarily intellectuals, but they received good educations, either at parish schools or from private teachers at home. A French traveller in the 19th century wrote that the Scots looked upon their wives as mortals and did not overwhelm them with compliments. They shared with their husbands the daily pains, pleasures and occupations of town and country life.

Girls from poorer backgrounds also had a measure of independence and those who lived in the country were often adept poachers. At the beginning of the 19th century Margaret Taylor was fined £1 at Perth for illegally taking salmon. Her

68 *'My First Capercailzie': a photo of Hilda Murray of Elibank from her book,* Echoes of Sport *(1910)*

plan was to set dogs trained for the purpose at the head of a fishing dam a little below the spawning bed of a river, while she sat several yards above in the neck of the stream, up to her hips in water, while her apron was stretched out under the water. At a signal the dogs dashed forward into the dam and drove the fish into the narrow water, where they had no alternative but to rush into the improvised net extended to receive them.

A crofter's daughter used cunning tactics to disarm suspicion on a grouse moor. The keeper had noticed, as the Twelfth approached, that his broods were diminishing, and he hid himself on the hill and watched. Before morning had far advanced his perseverance was rewarded. The smoke began to rise from the chimney of the thatched cottage of the nearest crofter, and presently he saw the crofter's daughter coming along, preceded by a collie, apparently to bring back some sheep, which had strayed over the march a few hundred yards further on. Now and then the dog would look up at his mistress, as if seeking permission to make himself useful. It was evident that they understood each other, as, no leave being yet accorded, the dog calmly trotted on in advance to the likely abode of a covey. Then at a sweep of the girl's hand off sped the collie over the moor, quartering his ground like a trained pointer. He stopped for a moment, poised himself and sprang, catching the rising grouse with scarcely a feather disturbed. The girl ran up, took the bird from his mouth and twisted its neck. The grouse then disappeared into the folds of the girl's dress, which was tucked up round her waist, and waving the dog again to work she advanced on her way to the march.

Another who took advantage of her sex, a farmer's daughter, was reputed to be one of the best shots in the Highlands. She had a little gun made for herself and used to roam the hills shooting grouse wherever she liked. The keepers used to wink at her poaching expeditions, the more so because she was particularly attractive. The laird of the estate went out with a party one day to find her blazing away ahead of them. They spread out and surrounded her; but she had evidently perceived their tactics, for when the party came up to her she was found to be busily gathering blaeberries, of which she had a large wickerwork basket nearly full. Her gun, presumably, she had hid somewhere in the heather. She brazened it out, though it must have required great nerve to offer blaeberries all round to the party of gentlemen looking at her with mingled amusement and admiration. The keeper could see grouse feathers sticking through the wickerwork beneath the covering of blaeberries, but he could also see that the laird did not want to convict the bold sportswoman, so he kept his tongue. As a gesture of chivalry, and to show that he was not altogether deceived, the laird sent the girl a small single-barrelled gun a few days afterwards addressed to her with his compliments.

Ladies of the landed class did not need to poach, but there were many who were skilled practitioners with a fishing rod, a number stalked and fewer used a shotgun. Those best known to us today are Lady Breadalbane, author of *The High Tops of Black Mount*, Diane Chasseresse, author of *Sporting Sketches*, and Mrs Murray of Elibank who wrote *Echoes of Sport*. It never has been the done thing for a woman to use a shotgun and that is as true today as it was in the late 17th century when Silvia in Farquhar's play, *The Recruiting Officer*, the prototype of Diana Vernon in *Rob Roy*, told her friend that she could 'gallop all the morning after the hunting horn and all the evening after the fiddle. In short I can do everything with my father but drink and shoot flying.' Only the most feminist of hosts in Victorian times would actually ask a woman to shoot, but hostesses quite frequently reserved to themselves the prerogative of participating. That in itself caused some misgiving: 'I shall be jealous if you meet the Duchess of Montrose at the Forest,' wrote Lady Eddisbury to her husband, and he agreed that he would be better pleased with her absence than her presence. Taking Duchesses to the hill did not improve the chance of success, he remarked, though she appeared quite at home among the horned beasts of the Forest.

Participants or not, and whatever ladies may have been thought of then or are thought of now as members of shooting parties, the most evocative description of moorland sport I have come across was written by a lady. I quote a letter written by Nina, Countess of Minto, to her husband on 23 August 1864:

My Dear Doddy,
We had two glorious days on the Moors. On the 12th William went up along with Berty, Hugh and Erskine Elliot; and on the 13th we took the whole party—hired post horses, had two open carriages filled with all young things, William and I being the only representatives of age, and a more successful day I never spent. It was as long as Joshua's, and the sun stood still over the moorland, while the moon was shining down on the valley of the Teviot. We saw the miracle performed, and shall never doubt it again. There were *no midges* that day, and nothing wanted to remind us of the imperfections of all earthly things *but you*. We drank to Lord John by the spring under the hill where he gave his famous toast in days gone by*; and then, after the party had dispersed, Arthur, Fitz and Fred to fish in Langhope Loch, which looked like a forget-me-not among the hills, and the others to shoot along the Burn, William and I decided

---

* Many years before, when a large family party were at Langhope, Lord John Russell startled the lunchers on the heather by proposing: 'May no one ever look back on this day with remorse!'

that we had solved the problem how to give the greatest happiness to the greatest number—to fill as many conveyances with as many young things as possible, and to transport them all for a long day at Langhope.

One charming consequence of outdoor recreations was the changes in fashion which ensued. 'I ask you,' said Sir John Astley, 'when do the fair sex look more bewitching than they do after a walk or drive to the luncheon tent . . . it is on these occasions that the well turned out walking-costume, with skirt short enough to prevent its draggling in the mud, treats you to a glimpse of the well-turned ankle and arched instep, and, perchance, the well-developed limb that keeps the stockings from wrinkling . . .'[2] Mrs Tweedie, in the novel *Wilton Q.C.*, which portrayed life in a Highland shooting-box for the interest of ladies left behind in London drawing rooms, described a party assembling for a day on the hill. The girls

> . . . were suitably dressed in serviceable tweeds. They wore gaiters over their thick boots, and any unprejudiced onlooker must have decided that a well-made shooting costume was really becoming. The very simplicity of the style tells, and a woman who is good looking, or who possesses a good figure, shows to quite as much advantage in her tweeds as she does in her habit. Jean looked particularly charming in one of the brown tweeds, heather dyed, made by her little crofter. She had a short kilt, which although it hung quite close to her figure, proved voluminous when required. It only reached a few inches below the knee, where it overlapped her knickerbockers, which in their turn joined her box-cloth gaiters.
> 'No petticoats for the moors, remember,' she said to Lorna, when explaining the costume she was to order. 'Knickerbockers, loose and warm, and confined at the knee by a band, where they meet the gaiters. Knickerbockers allow a freedom of gait no other garment can give. And mind, Lorna, good strong boots are all important. Thin boots mean bad colds, and bad colds mean no fun.'[3]

For dress not to be cumbersome was necessary not only for the comfort of the wearer but also for the convention that ladies must not be manhandled. Accounts of the period seem to indicate that it was de rigueur for servants, for example, to carry ladies over burns or rivers to prevent them getting their feet wet, but for gentlemen to lay hands upon them was compromising. Hence Sir John Astley

> had been told by my host to get through or over a treble wire fence into the park from a shrubbery, and I at once, with some difficulty, scraped through between

the wires, when my fair companion (one of the very best) essayed to follow me, and I strolled on while she made the attempt to coax her garments through the narrow aperture, but was roused from my reverie by a shrill voice of agony imploring me to help, as she could neither get backwards or forwards. Of course I put down my gun and rushed to the fair one's assistance, and, taking a firm grip of what I believed to be the tailor-made skirt, I, with considerable effort, landed its possessor in the field; but instead of grateful thanks, I dropped in for an awful wigging: 'How dare you! Only my husband would be allowed to do that, etc. etc.' and it was not till I explained to the lady that, unless I had rescued her, she would have been a fixture in all probability and brought in the next morning with the 'pick-up', that she burst out laughing and forgave me straight off. Of course I ought to have been more particular in selecting the substance that I grasped.[4]

Ladies out shooting were thought by Mr Punch to be a suitable subject for derision, and a shooting costume was illustrated in 1846 which anticipated Mrs Bloomer by a number of years. The supposed danger of women with guns also made them targets for ridicule. 'Call that silly dog of yours,' a keeper commanded, whose dog is on point. 'Can't you see he's standing right in my way?' And an account of the opening of the partridge season reads, 'Our bag on the First was barely up to the average, although the mater, Milly and self were out to help the men. We hunted in couples and threes, as it is a bit dull tramping along alone. And as the mater generally foozles her shots, I did most of her work too. By the way, how absurdly nervous men are gunning.'

In spite of the satire and the misgivings the ladies were by general consent, as Herbert Byng Hall gallantly expressed it as early as the 1840s, 'a charming addition to the delights of a shooting excursion, as in all other places and at all other times'.[5] The autumn holiday on the moors assumed its place as an accepted annual event of social and family life, and the idea that town life could be endurable again only came when 'the pinch of frost is to be felt in the air; a good many of our friends have gone to southern latitudes, and the girls, on the plea that they have almost nothing to wear, express their longing for a day's shopping in Regent Street. Ten weeks without shopping! Could anything testify more decidedly to the attractions of Glendower than to find a mother and daughters abstaining from the usual occupation for that lengthened period?'[6]

69 Driving Blackgame, *an illustration by J. G. Millais (1865– 1931) from his book*,
Game Birds and Shooting-Sketches (*1892*)

CHAPTER II

Bye Days

. . . after you have gone out and killed your fourteen or fifteen brace daily, fed under a sheltering birch-tree, as the magazine story-writers have it, and 'flasked' at the purling mountain stream, you have got right down the card, and there's nothing left for you to do.
Fores's Sporting Notes and Sketches, *1898*

When, as someone said in the smoking room of the lodge at Mealbannock one evening, there's a sameness in this grouse shooting, just a case of tramp, tramp, o'er moor and fell,[1] then it's time for a change.

Few moors are so placed as to lack the amenity of providing some sport other than grouse-shooting. Adventure may lie among the birch and spruce trees that shelter the lodge, with blackgame and roe deer, or upon the hills which rise above the heather slopes, the land of ptarmigan. There is sure to be a river or a burn to satisfy the angler, and if the moor lies beside the sea there is recreation for the yachtsman too.

On a wet or misty day a leisurely hour or two among the corn stooks in the afternoon was a pastime which yielded some variety of sport and pleased the farmer whose corn was suffering. From his hide of corn sheaves Sir John Astley once counted fifteen grouse, twelve partridges, six blackcock and some greyhens, five or six pigeons, two rabbits, a small stag and three hinds, all feeding within a hundred yards of him. The thing to do, rather unsportingly, was to line the birds up along the barrels of the gun and see how many could be killed with one shot. In such manner was a record once achieved, original both in its method of commemoration as well as in its achievement for it is engraved on the tombstone of a country churchyard. The inscription does not deal much with the past life or future hopes of the gentleman it commemorates, but simply records the fact that 'the deceased on one occasion killed 40 grouse at one shot'. This he achieved by taking an angled shot at a pack perched on a stone dyke.

That feats of shooting should be inscribed on tombstones emphasises the prestige of the grouse, and another tombstone in the churchyard of Bewcastle in

Cumberland commemorates Jonathan Telford of Craggyford, who died on 25 April 1866, aged seventy-two: 'Deceased was one of the moorgame shooters in the North of England; in the time of his shooting he bagged 59 grouse at seven double shots.'

The blackcock was the most prized bird in the corn stooks, and a day at blackgame among the birches on the fringe of the moor could be another rewarding sport when the hill was wreathed in mist. It might be a stalk along a peat hag or stone dyke, an impromptu drive or even a full-scale day's driving, for the shooting of driven blackgame was a practice perhaps more hallowed by time than driven grouse. In 1869, 247 were killed in a day at Glenwharrie in Dumfriesshire, and in 1870, 148 were killed on Elliock moor in the same county. The record, however, goes to Cannock Chase in Staffordshire, where 252 were killed one day in 1860. One of the guns, Lord Berkeley Paget, killed 126, which is in itself an unsurpassed feat.

On the high tops, ptarmigan had increased as eagles and hawks had been shot and the wild cat practically exterminated. Mountain hares increased for the same reason, and from time to time a beat would be organised over a wide tract of the country, each shooting tenant bringing his own tail of gillies. A sad fact was that the hill hare found little favour with game dealers. As for the sport, the hare has

70 Where Are They? *by Thorburn. Ptarmigan on the high tops*

little to recommend it, the pleasure lies mostly in the social occasion than the shooting, and it is a pity to see these creatures shot. With ptarmigan, the problem is to get a shot at all. Innes Shand said he saw little in ptarmigan-shooting to recommend; what he went for was the scenery and the sublimity of the views, and even in the walk itself there was the inherent risk of a sprained ankle or even a broken leg. When the day was still and the weather settled the shooting was comparatively tame, the birds either sitting like stones or running among the rocks like redleg partridges. When the wind was boisterous he settled for the view and went home.[2] But for Hesketh Prichard the difficulty of getting a shot was the challenge:

> Sometimes it is possible to drive ptarmigan, but as far as my experience goes, this is merely a matter of getting one or two shots. The line of flight of a covey is by no means certain, and the deer-stalkers do not pay much attention to its direction. Why should they? It is only once in three years or so that some crack-brained sportsman desires a day's ptarmigan shooting after the stalking season. Still, these impromptu drives are, to my mind, more interesting than the set drives of the lower lands. I yield to no one in my joy in a day's ptarmigan driving, for—especially as I grow older—my mind goes back with just as much,

71 On the Wall *by Thorburn. A favourite resting place for blackgame*

perhaps more, pleasure to the little days, when one lurked behind a rock and a single attendant drove the top.[3]

If, in the strath below the peaks, a salmon or trout river ran, the angler would find all the respite from grouse-shooting he desired. And if the land boasted only a burn or two, there was joy enough.

I know few things pleasanter in the way of fishing [wrote Lord Granby] than to wander amongst Highland hills, wherever some wee burn may run, Cairngorm-coloured, making miniature cascades over the boulders, or gliding quietly over pools which from the intensity of their colour seem trebly deep, equipped with a light, somewhat stiff rod, some Stewart tackle, and a bag of well-scoured brandling worms. . . . Are you not, as far as your personal ideas are concerned, monarch of all you survey? Probably you do not own an inch of all the glorious country around you, but you have leave to fish this particular burn, and that fills your cup of happiness. It is equally probable that, in giving you permission, the owner of the property looks upon you as a species of harmless lunatic, for the smallness of the stream and of the fish in it can be attractive only to a keen trout fisherman. But what does that matter to you? . . . So put on the Stewart tackle, double hooked (for the burn is small), without any shot on the cast, as the weight of the hook and its accompaniments suffices. And now as to the bait. You have in your basket a box of tough, not too large, brandling worms, which have been for a day or two in fresh moss and have thus had time to clean and harden themselves. Also you have, attached to a waist-coat button, a small canvas or brown holland bag with a thin wire run round the lip of its mouth, so as to keep it open sufficiently to enable you to put in your finger and thumb when you want a fresh worm.[4]

For those who were more gregarious and sought the sensational, the autumnal, nocturnal burning of the water was no doubt very picturesque. It is known as 'burning' because it is done in darkness with the aid of torches. The human figure is invisible beyond the light, and the light invites the fishes' curiosity. The usual result is a lot of salmon being caught which are so red as to be almost unfit for eating. Queen Victoria described the scene in 1850:

We walked with Charles, the boys, and Vicky to the river side above the bridge, where all our tenants were assembled with poles and spears, or rather 'leisters', for catching salmon. They all went into the river, walking up it, then back

72 *Salmon-fishing in the Highlands in the 1860s, from a drawing by M. S. Morgan*

again, poking about under all the stones to bring fish up to where the men stood with the net. It had a very pretty effect; about one hundred men wading through the river, some in kilts with poles and spears, all very much excited. Not succeeding the first time, we went higher up, and moved to three or four different places, but did not get any salmon; one or two escaping. Albert stood on a stone; and Colonel Gordon and Lord James Murray waded about the whole time. Duncan in spite of all his exertions yesterday, and having besides walked to and from the gathering, was the whole time in the water . . .

A salmon was speared here by one of the men; after which we walked to the ford, or quarry, where we were very successful, seven salmon being caught, some in the net, and some speared. Though Albert stood in the water some time he caught nothing; but the scene at this beautiful spot was exciting and pictur-esque in the extreme. I wished for Landseer's pencil.[5]

73 *The angler's dream. An illustration engraved on wood by E. Whymper from E. Lennox Peel's* A Highland Gathering (*1885*)

The salmon population suffered much from poaching at the mouths of rivers carried out by yachts. In the 1880s yachts increased greatly in number. Cruising on the west coast was popular from June onwards and the crews, sometimes under the direction of the owner or hirer himself, sometimes without his knowledge, dragged the mouths of the rivers at night and carried off the few fish that escaped the bag nets. Before morning the yachts had generally disappeared, and although gamekeepers often kept watch through the night and occasionally caught them in the act, yet many escaped in the dark nights, having cleared out if the season was dry, nearly the whole river's supply of fish, which was waiting at the mouth for a spate to ascend and spawn. As there were over 5,000 yachts in the United Kingdom—and the west coast of Scotland and the Hebrides were their favourite cruising grounds—it was obvious that such law-breaking could have very serious consequences for the owners of fisheries. Sometimes it was possible for a bay to be protected by large stones placed about it armed with iron hooks which fouled the nets, or similarly, illustrative of grouse shooters' drinking habits, champagne cases, filled with stones and spiked with nails, were sunk at strategic places.

West coast sport was rich in its variety, and anything was considered fair game for the gun. Codling, whiting and saithe were the most plentiful saltwater fish,

74 The Gentle Art: *an illustration from* Angling and Art in Scotland (*1908*) *by Ernest Brigs*

ERNEST BRIGGS

75 *A time that will be remembered. Fishing the River Leven near Kinlochbeg*

and for the gun there was the otter, porpoise, seal, wild birds on migration and rock pigeons to pursue. The latter frequented coastal and inland caves. They were not only difficult to shoot but also difficult to flush from their roosts owing to the noise of the waves on the rocks. Often nothing less than the firing of a gun would dislodge them, after hurling pieces of rock down the cliff had failed.

The killing of otters, seals and porpoises is not universally admired as sport today, nor was it then. Porpoises were often harpooned, generally unsuccessfully, and repulsive wounding was the outcome. Seals were a difficult quarry too, for they seldom rest on the shore of the mainland, preferring the greater safety of the points of small islands, where it was nearly always impossible to stalk them. The shooting of otters was more successful and also more defensible, for there was a big coastal population which harmed fishings. The method of shooting was to row from island to island with a couple of Skye terriers, visits being paid to every holt. The dogs were put into a hole well above the one opening into the sea, and if the otter was at home the dogs gave tongue at once.

A welcome feature of the pursuit of wildlife was that as time went on more people enjoyed doing it with a camera rather than a gun. It was not an easy task,

76 *Water-babies in Loch Leven, 1899*

for early cameras had a huge viewfinder and hood on top of the box, and when the photographer stalked wildfowl, deer or seals on his stomach it was almost impossible to get his head high enough to look into the viewfinder without being seen. Sunday afternoon was a suitable time, provided one's religious principles allowed it, to take photographs of the house party. By legend it was also, maddeningly for sportsmen, the one sunny day of the week. 'Have you had any fine days here during the last three months?' an exasperated tenant asked his gillie. 'Aye,' he replied, 'we've had four fine days and three was snappit up by the Sabbath.'

If the day was pleasant the midges could be an ordeal, for photography was a long and exacting performance when it started in the 1840s. The sitters had to stay motionless for eight minutes during exposure while the cameraman was enveloped in black velvet cloth. For those ambitious to photograph scenery a pony and pack saddle were necessary to convey the equipment up the hills. But technical progress was rapid; Archer's collodian process shortened exposure fifteen times and both optician and camera-maker improved photographic appliances radically by the 1850s.

Today nearly everybody has a camera, but in the Victorian era the visit of the itinerant professional photographer was a feature of the holiday. Lord Malmesbury noted in his memoirs that at Achnacarry in 1859 'Mr Ogle, the photographer, arrived, and made some excellent photographs of the beautiful scenery and of our party.' Another time at Dunvegan Vernon Heath, a pioneer photographer, remarked that the Bishop of Argyll and the Isles was liberal enough to allow him to photograph the house party on a Sunday and insisted on being included. Lord Aberdare, one of the group, remarked to his neighbour Sir Stafford Northcote, then Chancellor of the Exchequer, that the best thing he could do for Mr Heath would be to exempt him for ever from paying income tax.

The paintbrush tended to be the prerogative of the ladies, and it was pleasant to cruise on the yacht and let them sketch. In William Black's novel, *White Wings*, Angus Sutherland sheathed the spikes of Mary Avon's easel with cork so that it should not mark the deck, and placed a chair for her under the lee of the foresail to shade her from the sun. There were picnics on the islands and gathering of wild flowers while the evenings, if spent on board, were occupied with cards, dominoes or chess. If sea-sickness threatened to spoil the idyll, resolute eating and drinking was recommended, and in particular an adequate amount of *brut* champagne. The problem of the revictualling was always a worry for yachtsmen on the west coast for shops were few and although tinned foods were already in existence they were not much used.

For those who wished to amuse themselves less stylishly and sample more indigenous sorts of sport there were ample opportunities. Who could resist this invitation, so typical of the Scots' endearing habit of making a special occasion of an opening, whether it be of a bowling green, football ground or fishing?

> Loch Lomond, April
> Dear Sir, Noin u are font of thowin a flee I rite to let u know that I am in good health, hoppin this will find u the sain. Thank God for his mersis, we oppen Loch Ard on Wednesday next, when there will be some goot fishin. I will meet you at Balloch at eleven on Tuesday.
>
> Yours trooly
> Rory McTaggart

A time-honoured pastime of country people was the hunting of the fox with terriers. As early as 1631 Lord Mar wrote from Stirling to Campbell of Glenurchay in the following terms:

> To my very loving cousin the Laird of Glenurchay.
> Loving Cousin,
> Being come in to stay in this town a good part of this winter, I think my greatest sport shall be the hunting of the fox, therefore I will earnestly entreat you to send me with this bearer a couple of good earth dogs.
>
> This is my first charge since your father died, and I pray you use me familiarly as I do you; for without ceremony, cousin, you shall not have a friend over whom you have greater power than over me. Your loving cousin to do you service.
>
> Mar
> What you send me, let it be good, although it should be but one.

By the latter half of the 18th century the increase of the value of sheep led to regular employment of a district fox-hunter all over the Highlands. Farmers, besides making him a yearly payment, were expected to feed his dogs when he was working on their land. He either worked alone with his pack, perhaps two or three couple of strong slow-hounds, a brace of greyhound with a dash of the lurcher in them and a miscellaneous tail of terriers; or the country folk gathered together to draw an area where the fox was likely to be and then placed guns to guard the approaches to the earth he would probably make for.

A sportsman visiting the Highlands received an invitation to attend the latter sort of occasion one morning from a local keeper:

Sir,—As my son Dugal will tell you eef you cannot reid my rite Lachie McFayden, the fox hunter, will be here to hunt my hill tomorrow night with his dogs. As you said you would like to see a good hunt I let you know as soon as pocbel. Tell Doogal if you will come. 'Donald McKinnon'. Bring your gun. A bottle of whiskey would be verra goot, and two was better than wan.

The great social event in the autumn calendar was the Northern Meeting, instituted by the Duchess of Gordon at the very beginning of the 19th century.

She had persuaded [wrote Elizabeth Grant in her memoirs] all the northern counties to come together once a year about the middle of October, and spend the better part of a week at Inverness. There were dinners in the evening; the mornings were devoted to visiting neighbouring friends and the beautiful scenery abounding on all sides. She had always herself taken a large party there, and done her utmost to induce her friends to do likewise—stray English being particularly acceptable, as supposed admirers of national beauties! No one with equal energy had replaced her; still, the annual meeting went on, bringing many together who otherwise might not have become acquainted, renewing old intimacies, or sometimes obliterating old grudges.[6]

The one day when few activities were countenanced, and certainly not sports and pastimes, was Sunday. Even a game of tennis would have offended the customs of the country, and fishing as well as shooting was forbidden by law.

Church worship usually began at 1 p.m. with a couple of hours of Gaelic devotion, followed by the English service directly afterwards. Before about 1870 the organ or 'kist o'whistles' was regarded as a sign of black popery and the precentor's tuning fork gave the note from which he endeavoured to run up the scale for the choirless congregation. The precentor who stood in a lower desk directly under the minister, had to be able to distinguish the metres of the psalms and have voice and ear enough to raise at least three or four psalm tunes. His repertoire was seldom extensive.

The dress of the men was usually black, and the women wore white caps on their heads. Young girls wore no bonnet, but had their hair braided or plaited and bound by a snood, a bit of velvet or ribbon placed rather low on the forehead and tied beneath the plait at the back. Few wore shoes or stockings, and the girls used to wash their hair in a solution made from the young buds of birch trees, which agreeably scented the church. Shepherds brought their dogs with them, which slept until the minister pronounced the benediction, when they made for the door knowing full well it was time to start home for dinner. The congregation likewise, who due to the late hour would have had sandwiches before they left home, returned for a substantial meal at tea time.

The constraints of the Sabbath could be used for the gain of the community. A reckless baronet who rented a shooting had been brought to book by the authorities for fishing and shooting on Sunday, and to prevent the public exposure which a prosecution would have inflicted upon him he privately paid a fine of £5 to the poor-box.

A story was told of how the lure of money bent the conscience even of a kirk elder. A boatowner, he naturally had his boat lying high and dry on the Sabbath. He could not be guilty of sailing it himself, it was said, or permitting others to do so, for any consideration. But two sportsmen decided to test him. They knocked at his cottage door one Sunday afternoon and expressed their anxiety to be ferried across immediately. If he would take five shillings for the use of his boat, they would see that it was safely returned, even if he could not see his way to accompany them to the other side of the loch. The elder seemed to hesitate, as if trying to square his duty to his position with proper regard for his pocket. He accomplished this by remarking that if they liked to steal away the boat they were welcome to it, adding, 'when ye get a bit oot I maun com doon to the bank and sweer at ye; and ye can jist pay me on Monday!'

Sydney Smith probably had Sabbatarianism in mind when he called Scotland 'that garret of the earth—that knuckle-end of England—that land of Calvin, oatcakes and sulphur'. But the country minister was a man who understood the needs of his flock, often cultivated his own glebe, was a good judge of sheep and cattle and bred his own stock. He was also not averse to participation in sport. The minister of a parish on the River Spey charged his verger to inform him whenever he saw a salmon in the pool beside the church. One Sunday as the service was about to begin a salmon appeared there. Notified by his watchful accomplice, the minister bided his time, announced at the appropriate moment that the congregation would sing the whole of Psalm 119, slipped out of the church and, it was reputed, hooked and landed the salmon before the singing was over.

Likewise the minister of Glenmarkie, whose company W. A. Adams enjoyed, and whom he described as a scholar and a gentleman, fished the salmon pool beside the manse every day after breakfast and after tea, no matter the state of water or weather, once up and once down for five or ten minutes. Another minister went to the assistance of Augustus Grimble, who had succumbed to the temptation of surreptitiously fishing on Sunday and was playing a salmon when he came on the scene. He gaffed it neatly for him, remarking 'It would indeed be a pity to lose so bonny a fish, but I shall be obliged if ye will not mention my interference in the matter.'

Thus there were but few places where days of rest for the grouse could not be spent on a variety of amusements by their pursuers. There were areas of sport which deteriorated towards the end of the century, such as where improving proprietors drained land and reclaimed snipe bogs, where tenants exercised their rights under the Ground Game Act and reduced the sport at hares and rabbits, and where freeholders on the shores of lochs secured themselves good supplies of trout. But no unselfish person could in equity condemn such acts, and as every landowner knows who both farms and employs a gamekeeper, the latter is often the protagonist of the rural community and in his view sport is constantly being sacrificed in the interests, and not necessarily the best interests, of farming.

PART FIVE

Arts of the Moor

CHAPTER 12

Painters in the Heather

Sport in art . . . is a manifold history, in which all that belongs to sport . . . is represented side by side with changing customs and costumes, and with a great many landscape interests which belong for ever to the gradual changes made in country life .
Walter Shaw Sparrow, 1922

Sir John Everett Millais was pre-eminently a portrait painter, and though he is remembered less for his sporting pictures and his landscapes, as a painting sports-man he influenced, through his hospitality, encouragement and teaching, a num-ber of contemporary painters. Descended from an old Norman family which had long been settled in Jersey, Millais became acquainted with Scotland through John Ruskin. The two first met in 1851, and two years later Millais went on a trip to Scotland with Ruskin and his wife. Far-reaching consequences ensued from that holiday, for in 1855 Millais married Euphemia Chalmers, the eldest daughter of George Gray of Bowerswell, Perth, who had obtained a decree of nullity of her marriage with Ruskin. The newly marrieds spent some time together at Annat Lodge, near Bowerswell, and in subsequent years Millais indulged his love of shooting and fishing with an autumn holiday in Scotland.

One who enjoyed Millais's hospitality was John Leech, illustrator of Surtees and creator of Mr Briggs, the cockney sportsman whose misadventures on the moors delighted the readers of *Punch*. Many of the cartoons had their origins in those Scottish holidays. One day Leech was walking the hills near Blair when he found himself in a deer drive face to face with the Duke of Atholl. Abused by the Duke in terms such as 'Vile Sassenach', he was glad to escape intact. Later, Millais prevailed on Leech to be formally introduced to the Duke and participate in a drive, but he was so overcome by the heat of the day he fell asleep in his shelter as a herd of stags passed by. Both incidents were duly immortalised. Leech's humour was sustained by a particular faculty for landscape; its gentleness was a refreshing development beyond the brutal caricatures of Gillray and Rowlandson.

A DECIDED OPINION

Proprietor of shootings (" in the course of conversation "). " Yes, but you know, Sandy, it's difficult to choose between the Scylla of a shy tenant, and the Charybdis of——"
Sandy (promptly). "Aweel! Gie me the siller, an' any-buddy that likes may hae the tither!"

The tempo and variety of Millais's holiday pleasures gave inspiration to artists and writers and solace to the weary and the bon viveur. His zest was epitomised in the tale, probably apocryphal, from Murthly Castle in 1881. A blackcock flew over him while he was painting; he dropped palette and brushes, seized his gun, shot the bird and resumed his painting. The story is unlikely because he was a man of intense concentration and would not be interrupted from the matter in hand. His son, J. G. Millais, said that he would have killed anyone who began to talk to him of pictures when his mind was running on salmon or grouse.

There were some nice touches for the cartoonist in the incidents that are revealed from Millais's letters. As he waited for the weather to improve he became exasperated not only by the rain but also by the greeting of 'It's a varry saaft dee,' every day for five weeks. And when it was fine the 'midges bit so dreadfully that it is beyond human endurance to sit quiet, therefore many a splendid day passes without being able to work'. At least the rain that fed the rivers afforded 'the most delightful baths, perfectly safe, and clear as crystal. They are so tempting that it is quite impossible to walk by them without undressing and jumping in'.

In his shooting Millais preferred the gun to the rifle and apparently never acquired great skill with the latter. Deer-stalking had too many hardships and disappointments for him: 'I am aching in all my limbs from having crawled over stony impediments in pursuit of a stag. I shall never forget the tail-between-legs dejection of that moment when the animal, instead of biting the dust, kicked it up viciously into my face.' He viewed with distaste the fact that the stalker so often ensured that the chance of a shot depended on the social rank of the shooter, and it was altogether a more pleasant thing to shoot his way up to the moor, spend the day painting, and return at evening with a brace or two of grouse and perhaps a blackcock, woodcock or snipe. When he asked friends to stay for the shooting he was meticulous on matters of safety, but his oft-repeated cautionary lectures went awry one day while the party of guns was crossing a turnip field. In the middle of

79 *Richard Ansdell, R.A.*, Midday Rest (*1849*)

the field was a cottage, and at one of the windows an old woman sat knitting. Firing at a partridge flying back, Millais killed the bird, peppered the old woman and smashed five panes of glass, all at one shot.

Shooting and painting were both good reasons for long stays in Scotland and Millais discovered, as other artists have discovered since, that it was a good country to paint in winter. 'This is much better than the Riviera,' he said as he gazed away to the north from Perth Bridge one bright winter morning, 'I can't see to paint in London in November.' The winter in Perthshire was usually open, and while the days were sadly short their brightness was a revelation to most southerners wintering there for the first time. At Rohallion, in the Tay valley, he got a local carpenter to build him a little hut on the high ground of the Trochray beat, where with his materials on the spot he could paint in comfort. He always recalled with pleasure the occasion when a gale and snowstorm raged down the valley and he feared for the safety of the hut in which he had left his picture *Christmas Eve, 1887*. In great anxiety he waited till the morning, expecting to find hut and contents blown away. To his delight it still stood, thanks to his carpenter friend who had gone at midnight in the blinding gale to make it thoroughly secure.

When the hours of work or sport were over and the winter evenings drew on, the long hours of darkness were no trial, for Millais's energy flowed on. There was the occasion when, as a guest of the Duke of Rutland at St Mary's Tower, he met Disraeli, the latter having broken his journey to Balmoral for a few days' rest at Dunkeld. Millais remarked what a very interesting talker Disraeli was, but it turned out that the great statesman, being so overcome by the fatigue of his journey had remained almost silent, while Millais had talked the whole evening. Millais expressed the hope that he would enjoy the quiet repose of St Mary's. 'Yes, I am already happy in this lovely spot. There are no Secretaries or Government bags here.'

Repose, too, was sought by George Du Maurier in the autumn of 1890. Troubled with his eyesight he took a long holiday as Millais's guest at Murthly Castle, accompanied by his daughter Sylvia. When weather permitted he went with the others to the moor or the river, and in the evenings, or at any odd times, he would enliven the gathering with little French chansons. The food was exquisite, superintended by Auguste Mazarin, a French chef of great excellence. He used to paint portraits of questionable beauty and was more proud of his artistic efforts in the studio (his bedroom) than of his success in the kitchen. When the subject of art was mentioned he commonly referred to 'Messieurs Millais et moi'. From Du Maurier's visit to Murthly was conceived the character of the Laird in *Trilby*, based on Millais.

Among others who enjoyed those Scottish holidays were two men whose writings and paintings enriched the art and literature of sport and natural history. In such an atmosphere it was appropriate that Sir John's son, J. G. Millais, should have conceived his great works on the natural history of British game birds and on diving and surface-feeding ducks. Lesser known is Archibald Stuart-Wortley, whose writings have charm, and who under the elder Millais's tuition became a sought-after portrait painter. He learned more from his tutor in a few short weeks, he said, than from all the other masters who from time to time directed or misdirected his artistic studies.

I would lay down my palette, and, going round to where he paced to and from his canvas, eager, absorbed, his eyes glittering like stars in the concentration of his gaze upon subject and picture, would exclaim 'I can't draw those leaves or grasses,' or whatever it might be. 'Dash it, my boy,' he would say, 'you must draw them. Remember that if you don't some fellow will come from round the corner who *will*.'[1]

A challenge which both young men did take up, and which Sir John Millais said he always wanted to do, was to paint a grouse drive. J. G. Millais did a number of examples, and Stuart-Wortley's painting *The Big Pack*, reproduced as an illustration in the monograph on grouse in the 'Fur and Feather' series, appropriately came to be owned by R. H. Rimington Wilson of Broomhead fame. To paint driven game is not an easy task, but if the paintings of these two artists may be criticised, principally because they over-dramatised the scene, the true depiction of the flight of grouse reflected their skill as draughtsmen and their knowledge of natural history. The same may be said of George Lodge, another contemporary artist and illustrator, who in his memoirs gave an example of the advantage of observation with the artist's eye. He used to

make a practice of making rough pencil sketches of the view from every grouse butt I occupied. There was almost always a long enough wait before the grouse began to come; also, on bye days, I used to toil up the hills with my painting kit and make oil sketches of grouse country. . . . I remember once painting a small picture for the late Edwin Montagu of some driven grouse. This he criticised, saying that he thought I had made their necks too long. I told him he might be right, but as he was going to Scotland shortly to shoot grouse, I asked him to take special notice of the point. This he did, and when he came back he said that after what he had just seen, he now thought I had not made the necks long enough![2]

The shooting of game over dogs presented a more attractive composition for artists and attracted the talent of Gainsborough, Stubbs, Marshall, Wheatley, J. N. Sartorius, Wootton, Howitt, Alken, Reinagle and John Leech—to name but a few. The Victorians had one great advantage over 20th-century artists; the costumes of those days lent colour which is missing from modern shooting clothes.

On his appropriately broad canvases no one depicted the elegance of the early Victorian grouse-shooting party on the moors better than Richard Ansdell. Born in Liverpool in 1815, Ansdell's first exhibited painting at the Royal Academy was *Grouse-Shooting—Luncheon on the Moors* in 1840. He excelled at the open-air scene on a grand scale and his pictures have a wider appeal than those of his pre-eminent rival in the Scottish sporting genre, Edwin Landseer. The latter, in fact, was uninterested in the portrayal of grouse-shooting because it was a rather middle-class sport, preferring deer-stalking with its aristocratic origins. His attitude was epitomised in his companion paintings *High Life* and *Low Life*, portraying the disdainful deerhound and the butcher's dog.

80 The Keeper's Boy (*1873*) *by James Hardy Jr.* (*1832–89*). *The design of the modern pony-pannier has in no way changed*

81 Early Grouse Driving *by Douglas Adams (op. 1880–1905). The kind of drive where accidents can happen. Even a high bird may be in line with the other guns*

Twentieth-century painters have enjoyed better access to the public with their work than their forebears, thanks to modern colour printing. The most notable example among artists of the moorland scene is Archibald Thorburn, whose pictures are familiar to every sportsman and naturalist. Born in Dumfries in 1860 he went to London as a young man and learned much of his skill from Joseph Wolf. The latter was a German by birth and an Englishman by adoption, and a master at painting both birds and animals. Doubly fortunate in his sources of influence, Thorburn became acquainted with the celebrated ornithologist Lord Lilford, whose *Coloured Figures of the British Birds* he illustrated in the 1890s. Lilford bestowed on him the highest praise, saying of one of his pictures that he had thrown into it 'an element of Highland poetry . . . that is not often attained . . .'

In that element of poetry lies the key to the success of Thorburn and Lodge as primarily bird painters; V. R. Balfour-Browne and Frank Wallace as deer painters; and Lionel Edwards as a painter of the hunting scene. For each not only portrayed the birds and animals with which they were well acquainted, but with equal knowledge the setting in which they lived and moved. These men were not only painters, but naturalists and sportsmen too, and the pursuit of shooting or stalking or hunting was as important a part of their life as their painting.

In this the painters of the last generation differed from their counterparts today who, with some notable exceptions, are studio painters. That is not to decry the skill of their work, but the majority of, for example, modern bird painters, are portrait painters who, working from skins, can portray with dazzling accuracy, the plumage of their subject. The bird is the thing, and fine it is too, but the landscape in which it lives is but a shadowy substance.

82 The Gathering Storm *by Thorburn. When bad weather comes, grouse will be wild and unapproachable*

83 The Shadow of Death *by Thorburn. The Golden Eagle is known to take full-grown grouse*

84 Grouse Driving in Aberdeenshire (*1977*) *by Rodger McPhail*

It would be unfair, though, to omit from mention three living painters of the grouse moor, namely J. C. Harrison, Philip Rickman and Rodger McPhail. Harrison's pictures of grouse on the wing show that he knows what it is all about and Rickman's likewise, though the latter's pictures of red grouse are not common. Blackgame are a favourite subject for him, and he excels in portraying them flying against a background of snowclad landscape, among the birch trees on the fringe of the moor. Rodger McPhail encouragingly, is a much younger man than these two, still only in his twenties. As much at home with a gun as with a paint brush, his pictures have the ring of truth.

CHAPTER 13

Fireside Tales

Late the next night, perchance, as one drives through the lighted streets and sees the placards of London and the white faces, the hum, the roar, the ten thousand solicitations of shop and theatre, one goes back in thought—the lodge is dark, the little round patch in front is soaked with dew, the loch reflects the stars. Far up, far up beneath them the grey geese are flighting from Cuirheara. *Hesketh Prichard*, Sport in Wildest Britain

The sporting literature of the 19th century may be divided into two categories: the books written by those who were country dwellers steeped in both the sport and the natural history of their subject; and the books written by holiday sportsmen who had something to tell their fellows of the practice of their sport, the problems they might encounter, the scenery, the fun and so on. A third category was the compendium written by the jack-of-all-sport and master of none, the most famous of which was the Revd. William B. Daniel's *Rural Sports*, published in three volumes in 1801. Daniel has little to say about the practice of grouse-shooting, but his medley of jumbled information and anecdote makes entertaining reading. The illustrations include engravings from Stephen Elmer, H. B. Chalon and Philip Reinagle. Elmer's pictures can always be recognised, with the necks and bodies of his birds distinctively elongated. He must have been a quite prolific artist for his pictures still come on the market often.

The most celebrated book on 19th-century Scottish sport, *Wild Sports and Natural History of the Highlands*, was published in 1845 and by coincidence the author, Charles St John, was at school with Thomas Jeans, whose satire *The Tommiebeg Shootings* had such a reforming influence on Highland landlords. From those early days St John steeped himself in the study of natural history:

> his box . . . was generally a sort of menagerie—dormice in the one till, stag-beetles of gigantic size and wonderful caterpillars in paper boxes in the other, while sometimes a rabbit, sometimes a guinea-pig, or perhaps a squirrel, was lodged below in a cell cunningly constructed of the Delphic classics and Ainsworth's Dictionary. He was scarcely without live-stock of some sort.[1]

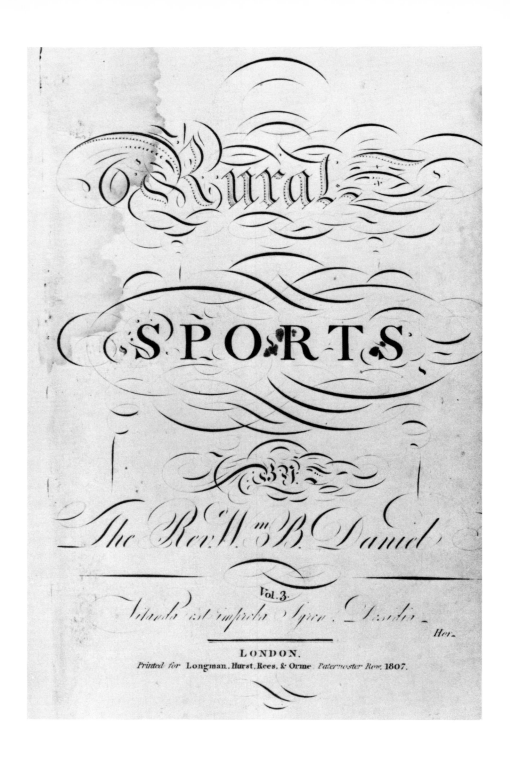

85 *A jumbled but most entertaining book, some of* Rural Sports *was written by Daniel when in King's Bench Prison, London, for debt*

After leaving school St John spent a few irksome years as a clerk in the Treasury until, in 1834, he married Anne Gibson. His bride was a lady of some fortune, which he lacked, and he was able to settle down at Rosehall in Sutherland to the life of a sportsman and naturalist. He was one of the old school who shot only for the pot, as he said deriving more satisfaction from

killing a moderate quantity of birds, in a wild and varied range of hill, with my single brace of dogs, and wandering in any direction that fancy leads me, than in having my day's beat laid out for me, with relays of dogs and keepers, and all the means of killing the grouse on easy walking ground, where they are so numerous that one has only to load and fire.[2]

Of the three books Charles St John wrote—*Sport in Moray*, *Tour in Sutherlandshire* and *Wild Sports and Natural History of the Highlands*—the last has since become a classic. No less a reputation was enjoyed by John Colquhoun's *The Moor and The Loch*, published in 1840. Both books ran to many editions over a long period of years; not only did their authors bring a new, scholarly approach to writing of the countryside, but they were also strenuous in defending creatures that seemed threatened with extinction such as the eagle and the badger by over-zealous game preservers. These writings are of unique interest to the present-day reader, for they described wild sport which progressively lessened as the century advanced. More intensive farming reduced the variety of sport on the fringe of the moor, winged predators disappeared as extravagant rewards were offered for them and fancy prices paid for their eggs, while manufacturing processes were already being set up whose residues would poison the salmon and trout in rivers.

While the books of writers such as St John and Colquhoun are of particular interest to the sportsman and naturalist, those written by holiday sportsmen have a wider interest. The person who goes to Scotland merely to explore the country can gain a lot of pleasure from works such as Herbert Byng Hall's *Highland Sports and Highland Quarters*, with its descriptions of people and places, inns and their bills of fare and the hazards and amusements of travelling. The fact that he was a newcomer to Scotland led him to set down details which a native of the country would have considered too minor to merit mention. The book appeared in the late 1840s, and was followed by a number of similar books in the 1880s, such as E. Lennox Peel's *A Highland Gathering* and Samuel Abbott's *Ardenmohr among the Hills*.

The book boom in Highland sport of the two closing decades of the century testified to the popularity of the pastimes they depicted and the books themselves are fine productions. Notable is *A Highland Gathering*, with its illustrations by

Charles Whymper. More opulent in size were the works of Augustus Grimble. In 1889 he was staying at Gaick where fortuitously he met Archibald Thorburn, who was there for a few days to study ptarmigan for Lord Lilford's *British Birds*. Through their meeting Thorburn's services were secured for illustrating Grimble's *Shooting and Salmon Fishing, Highland Sport* and *The Deer Forests of Scotland*. Between that time and his death in 1935 Thorburn illustrated a host of books, but none better than A. E. Gathorne-Hardy's *Autumns in Argyleshire with Rod and Gun*.

Unlike the few books written by occasional sportsmen earlier in the century Gathorne-Hardy depicted a scene which he had long known, and which therefore he was able to describe in historical perspective and in great variety. His memory, he wrote,

> carries me back over thirty years, every autumn of which has been spent in the North. There are few parts of Scotland, from Sutherland to the Border, which have not echoed to the report of my gun. What varieties of scene, what differences of climate, flit across the mind's eye at the thought of the first day of the season; tropical heat, arctic cold, light breezes and shifting clouds; thunder and lightning and torrents of rain; the round rolling hills of Ross-shire; the Perthshire tablelands, so easy to walk after the hard climb to get to them; the broken mountains of Argyle with their succession of small hills and valleys and constantly recurring visions of blue sea and distant islands; the down-like Border country, intersected by Esk, Teviot, and Dryfe, and rich with a thousand memories of Christopher North and Sir Walter.[3]

Many shared the breadth of Gathorne-Hardy's experiences and wrote about them with varying literary ability, but to do more than merely list their works in the bibliography would occupy too much space. One aspect of the sporting literature of the time must however be mentioned, and that is the different series on sport which appeared. First of them was the Badminton Library, published in the 1880s, the volumes of which dealt with every major sport and which was the forerunner of many 'libraries' of sport since. Notable have been the 'Fur, Feather and Fin' series of monographs on game animals, birds and fishes in the 1890s; 'The Gun at Home and Abroad', published in 1912 and dedicated to King Edward VII; and the 'Lonsdale Library', published in the 1930s. The first is, to my mind, the most delightful of all these ambitious publications, combining sound knowledge with literary excellence and pleasing illustrations. The volume, *The Grouse*, was written by the Revd. H. A. Macpherson and Archibald Stuart-Wortley; the former treated the natural history of the subject and the latter the

86 Mr Punch in the Highlands (*1905*). *Through the pen of such artists as Charles Keene, G. D. Armour and John Leech,* Punch *satirised Highland sports*

shooting. Stuart-Wortley also shared the illustrating with Thorburn, but the vivid tempo of his prose brought the excitement of the Twelfth to life as almost no picture could do.

The thrill of anticipated pleasures starts first, he says, as the lamps are being lit in Bloomsbury and the cab rattles along towards Euston or King's Cross. As the train draws out of the station you rouse yourself to

> pull down the window for a moment to sniff an air that blows fresher and sweeter than St Stephen's, Capel Court, Lincoln's Inn, or Pall Mall, and to become aware that you are tearing over the borders of Hertfordshire at forty-

87 *Published in the 1890s, the* Fur, Feather and Fin *Series is the most delightful of all the 'libraries' of field sports ever published*

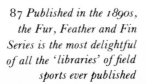

five miles an hour, on a magnificent starlight night. The great oaks and elms of old England fleet by you like streams of cardboard trees, the long, low landscape fades into the blue-black of the sky, and so steady is the going that the distance seems like a slow dioramic procession of woods and hills, while you alone are motionless, and the nearer objects—houses, fences, telegraph poles, parapets, or platforms—but so many formless phantoms, rushing with roar, scream, and rattle back to the South.[4]

By next morning you are among the hills and

in this glorious amphitheatre you attack your sport. The white dog comes to a dead point on your side of a knoll, and is beautifully backed by the liver-coloured bitch, who halts on a great piece of flat rock some seventy yards away, a motionless and perfect picture. Three grouse rise, you kill with your first, and, your host courteously waiting to let you deal with your first right and left alone, strike the second hard but underneath, while he neatly drops the third bird—a beautiful long cross shot.[5]

When the day is far spent and tracks are made for home,

turning out of the wood you come upon all the glory of the yellow moon, just rising over the eastern hill, and glittering in the waters of the loch; the horses quicken their pace, lights twinkle in the distance, and now as you swing in at the gate of the lodge grounds a savoury whiff courts your nostrils from the shining kitchen window, while as you turn the corner to the door the first skirl of the pipes warns you that it is already half-past eight, the ladies are waiting, and you must be quick down to dinner.[6]

Of 20th-century writers on sport who provide a link with Victorian times the most notable has been Osgood MacKenzie, creator of the gardens at Inverewe and author of *A Hundred Years in the Highlands*. The book was first published in 1921, when Osgood was seventy-nine, and it combined his own reminiscences with those of his uncle, Dr John MacKenzie, who left behind him ten manuscript volumes of *Highland Memories* covering the period 1803 to 1860. It is essential reading for anyone wishing to understand the social life of the Highlands in the 19th century, and in no other book are field sports better described in the context of country life.

Numerous books devoted to grouse-shooting have been produced over the past

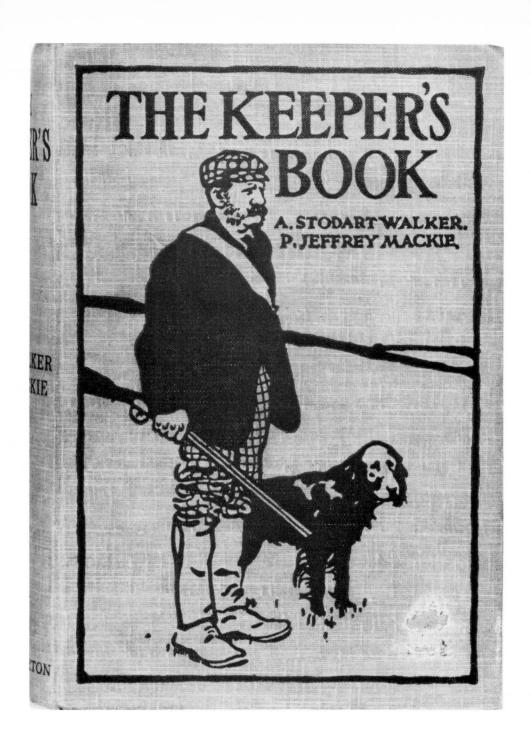

88 *As the gamekeeper's work became more skilled, it was fitting that by 1904 he should have a handbook of his tasks*

few decades by such writers as Bernard Cazenove, Lord George Scott, J. K. Stanford and Martin Stephens. These tend to be textbooks, and for the pleasures of shooting one must turn elsewhere. For bedside reading I commend Lionel Edwards's *My Scottish Sketch Book*, published in 1929, a collection of paintings of shooting, fishing, hunting and stalking with apt notes on the illustrations. More prolific with the pen, and incidentally a collaborator with Edwards on a book on deer-stalking and another on the scenes of the Forty-five was the fellow artist Frank Wallace. In *Happier Years*, *A Highland Gathering*, *Hunting Winds* and *Please Ring the Bell*, Wallace recalled the past with absurd and rather tiresome nostalgia but much wit. Deer were his abiding love, both to paint and to stalk, but in his four books of recollections there are some entertaining vignettes of grouse shooting.

I have already described *The Tommiebeg Shootings*. But one other work of fiction, written at the end of the century, captures inimitably the humour of shooting. There is a chapter in *The Irish R.M. Stories* entitled 'The Shooting of Shinroe' which features a nameless red setter, which accompanied Major Yeats and Mr McCabe,

> . . . a large dog, with a blunt stupid face, and a faculty for excitement about nothing that impelled him to bound back to us as often as possible, to gaze in our eyes in brilliant inquiry, and to pant and prance before us with all the fatuity of youth. Had he been able to speak, he would have asked idiotic questions, of that special breed that exact from their victim a reply of equal imbecility . . . Once a small pack of grouse got up, very wild, and leagues out of range, thanks to the far-reaching activities of the dog, and once a hermit woodcock . . . sailed away down the slope, followed by four charges of shot and the red setter, in equally innocuous pursuit. And this, up to luncheon time, was the sum of the morning's sport.
>
> We ate our sandwiches on a high ridge, under the lee of a tumbled pile of boulders, that looked as if they had been about to hurl themselves into the valley, and had thought better of it at the last moment. . . . The dog sat opposite to me, and willed me to share my food with him. His steady eyes were charged with the implication that I was a glutton; personally I abhorred him, yet I found it impossible to give him less than twenty-five per cent of my sandwiches.

Several 20th-century novels concern themselves with shooting. *Ben Watson*, written by C. J. Cutliffe-Hyne, and published in 1926, is set in the north of

England and is a racy tale revolving primarily around grouse-shooting. The only novel devoted entirely to the grouse was published in 1944. The author, J. K. Stanford, wrote several novels on a shooting theme but *The Twelfth* is his classic. Anyone who has not read it should acquaint himself with the metamorphosis of George Proteron, and all the adventures he was involved in, such as the shocking accident on the Banchovie Moor, in which Lord Charles Casserole was knocked senseless by a driven grouse, and in falling fatally injured both his loader and the next gun.

Pride of place to writers on field sports in this century must go to Patrick Chalmers. Born in 1875, son of the laird of Aldbar in Angus, his prose and verse delighted readers of *Punch* and *The Field* for more than forty years, and his thirty or more books included biographies of J. M. Barrie and Kenneth Grahame. He was steeped in classical lore and Highland mythology and could depict in whimsical manner the scene and characters of moor, forest or river. A merchant banker by profession, the fact that he was born on the business side of the Border is illustrated by the story of how, as a young man who had published some light verse in various periodicals, he was asked if he would like to be introduced to a publisher. 'How much do I pay?' he replied.

The poem which conjures up the lure of the North most magically is 'Euston'. Here is the opening:

> Now, when the sportsman is flitting from market and Mammon,
> Now, when the courts, swept and garnished, stand silent and lone,
> Now, with her challenging grouse, and her sea-silver salmon,
> August, of mountains and memories, comes to her own;
> Would you gaze into the crystal, and see the long valleys,
> Braes of the North, and the rivers that wander between,
> Crags with whose coating the tint of the ptarmigan tallies?
> Come up to Euston tonight about 7.15.[7]

89 *Christmas fare: the scene outside a poulterer's shop in Holborn, London, in 1845*

CHAPTER 14

Dining on Grouse

Now may no reader of this book ever have to buy game! Let him for ever take it home with him, as an appurtenance or as a gift, on the evenings of happy shooting days.
Patrick Chalmers, The Shooting-Man's England

On the shelves of our library at Cromlix is a row of books which has some bearing on our guests' enjoyment. These are the cookery books and folders of cookery recipes accumulated by my grandfather during his fifty years here. The pages on grouse are well thumbed and much can be learned from them concerning the development of cooking. Similarly, from some of the other old books on sport the history of game consumption and the game trade can be deduced.

Game preservation in Scotland, other than in the royal forests, dates back little more than 200 years. So long as a person had the necessary qualifications to own a licence to kill game, no one had a right to challenge him for trespass, because Scottish game laws were founded on Roman law. In isolated rural districts game was plentiful, the people helped themselves, and landlords took scant notice. A tenant farmer was often only too glad to have a townsman visit him with a gun for a few days, bringing possibly as his shooting rent £1 for his wife, some sweets for his children and some tobacco, snuff and whisky for himself. The landlord had no reason to interfere with a custom harmless to himself and of benefit to his tenant.

In less remote areas it came to be an entirely different matter when whole bands of townsmen, the equivalent of motorised poaching gangs today, invaded the moors armed with old Queen Anne muskets and accompanied by packs of village dogs. These mobs did a great deal of mischief by damaging trees, knocking down stone walls, disturbing sheep and otherwise upsetting the harmony of the countryside. The coopers of Leith and Edinburgh with numerous fish hawkers and fish porters used to proceed regularly to the Fife shore in this fashion from the ancient fishing port of Newhaven and return with boats laden to the gunwale with the spoils of the chase. In the 1760s, when these poaching mobs became a menace,

Scottish landlords intimated that poachers holding no licence would be prosecuted on unenclosed moorlands, and 'duly qualified gentlemen' were requested to keep away. Thus the Duke of Buccleuch advertised as Lollino in the *Edinburgh Evening Courant* in 1767, 'that the game on his Grace the Duke of Buccleuch's estates in the south of Scotland having been greatly destroyed of late by poachers and others not entitled to game, his Grace has appointed gamekeepers, who are authorised to prosecute all offenders in terms of law, and it is hoped no gentleman will offend'.

Harsher sanctions against poaching resulted from the assimilation of Scottish game laws with English in the 1850s and their contrast with the earlier liberality evoked sympathy for the poacher. Meg Dods looked back with nostalgia to the old lairds who were

> . . . decent, considerate men that didna plague a poor hard callant muckle about a moorfowl or a mawkin*, unless he turned common fowler—Sir Robert Ringhorse used to say, the herd lads shot as money gleds† and pyots‡ as they did game. But new lords new laws—naething but fine and imprisonment, and the game no a feather the plentier. If I wad hae a brace or two of birds in the house, as every body looks for them after the twelfth—ken what they are like to cost me—and what for no?—risk maun be paid for.—There is John Pirner himself, that has keepit the muir—side thirty year, in spite of a' the lairds in the country shoots, he tells me, now-a-days, as if he felt a rape about his neck.

In the early 19th century the increase in poaching, and more stringent game laws, were symptomatic of a developing trade in game. Grouse were sent to London by boat, and delays were such that they were often unsaleable by the time they arrived. But with the advent of railways the epicure could have his bird on the Twelfth in prime condition. Grouse were snared or netted a few days beforehand and sent to London and Manchester by train, packed in herring barrels or salmon boxes, such packages being known to railway officials as 'fish with feathers on them'.

Thousands of birds obtained illicitly were sent to markets in this manner, and by the middle of the century there were fears that the consequent scarcity of grouse would lead to tenants giving up their sporting leases. Keepers on moorlands which were netted by poachers drove in stakes to thwart them, but it was less easy to catch the small farmer or shepherd who set horsehair nooses on his sheaves of corn.

* Hare.　　† Buzzards.　　‡ Magpies.

The unfortunate effects of this trade were that moors were harmed, the poacher got a poor price for his goods, and game legally obtained fetched a deflated price owing to the market being flooded. At the same time a huge import trade in ptarmigan from Norway, packed in ice as ballast for empty vessels, increased the game supply. Nevertheless, the price of game was high in relation to what it fetches nowadays. The average price of grouse in the 1880s was about 8s a brace with a peak price of 25s at the beginning of the season. About half a million grouse and blackgame were said to have been sold annually.

On the table the grouse has never in fact equalled the prestige it enjoyed in mid-Victorian times. The indigenous creatures of the countryside were symbols of civic luxury and simple food was fashionable. The old London eating-houses, typified by Stone's in Panton Street, Gow's in the Strand and Rule's in Maiden Lane, catered for the great nation of meat-eaters. It was no coincidence that a steep fall in the price of game occurred in the 1880s when distrust and dislike of foreigners, reflected in ignorance of and indifference to French cooking began to abate. The opening of the Savoy in the late '80s marked a new era in the history of London restaurants. Ladies had begun to acquire a measure of independence: they enjoyed being seen and admired in public; they were less conservative than men in their taste; they were eager to dine out and taste new dishes. From Europe came restaurateurs eager to satisfy their whims—Frascati, Maxim, Pinoli.

Middle-class enthusiasm for foreign foods can be observed by reference to the cookery books of the period, in which a miserable amount of space was accorded to game. Only in the homes of the aristocracy did English cookery still retain its excellence and the aristocracy did not use cookery books. At least, their cookery books were their own compilations, handed down through generations of cooks, added to, gleaned from friends and neighbours, sometimes privately printed. Anyone who has lived in a Victorian house which has not been 'turned out' will have come across these fascinating collections of recipes, mingled with still valuable hints on household management.

In the world at large the grouse suffered from not only the vagaries of taste but also from the cold storage trickster, who has now practised his deceit for a century. The bird that was heralded on the magic day as having been brought direct from the moors had either been a frozen carcass a few hours before or was killed out of season. No doubt, too, the ptarmigan carried as ballast in ships from Norway masqueraded as their red relations. Fast forms of transport nowadays make deception less likely, but caution is still necessary. Sir Winston Churchill's rejection once of roast grouse in favour of steak-and-kidney pie in a London restaurant on the Twelfth was probably wise.

He knew exactly what was happening in London. The morning papers, especially *The Times*, would all be carrying special articles on the Twelfth, and the cheaper ones would inevitably prefix the word 'glorious' or refer somehow to the 'Feast of Saint Grouse'. There would be portraits (there had been of George in years gone by) of great ones 'in the butts' in the very act of slaughter. In the evening papers next day someone would be sure to write that 'on all the principal moors sportsmen were early astir' (though George himself in other years had always firmly declined to be astir before 7.15). And some oaf, who probably hailed from Whitechapel, was bound to commit a *gaffe* about the 'crack of the rifle' being heard on the moors. Poulterers in Leadenhall and Jermyn Street and in the vaults of the Savoy had already, George felt certain, blast them! the hundreds of brace of young grouse hanging on hooks which officially would be shot and 'flown to London' next day in time to grace the luncheon of despicable stockbrokers and attorneys and others whom no one had ever asked to shoot. (J. K. Stanford, *The Twelfth*, p. 48.)

Modern cookery books devote more space to game, indeed are often entirely concerned with game, but recipes for grouse are rarely as numerous as for other birds or beasts. For that there is good reason. George Saintsbury, author of the delightful essay on grouse cookery in the 'Fur, Feather and Fin' series, praised a hostess who had prepared for him 'very few things for dinner today; for there is grouse, and I think grouse is a dinner'. Simple roasting is all that is necessary for a young bird to be excellent; dryness is the only enemy, and that can be guarded against by jackets of bacon, larding and aluminium foil.

For full instructions on the roasting of a young grouse there is no one better than H. B. C. Pollard, author of that now rare work, *The Sportsman's Cookery Book*:

Sprinkle inside with spiced pepper, salt, peppercorns, and dried herbs pounded together in a mortar. Insert a 1-inch cube of butter or a spoonful of clear bacon fat. While roasting baste liberally with bacon fat or run butter. The drippings should be absorbed on a square of toast set below the bird either under the turnspit or, if they are oven roast, in the roasting tin. This toast is brought to the table with the bird on it.

Fried breadcrumbs, bread sauce and a little made gravy are served with the bird, which should be garnished with watercress. Claret is the appropriate wine, and French beans the accompanying vegetable.[1]

For those who like to have a little jelly with their grouse, Providence has so ordered things that the fruits of the hills are in harmony. The cranberry and rowanberry are good, and whortleberries and bilberries are sometimes used for stuffing. Salmon is an excellent prelude to the main course; Saintsbury had a friend who kept a supply of grouse hanging till he could accompany them with salmon caught in a river which was by no means a very early one, and the birds never tasted better. To complete the meal a gooseberry fool is perfect.

Patrick Chalmers was in accord with that plan when he imagined his dream dinner:

> I cannot but think that the principal plat will be game—grouse for me—since I wish to dine, wide-windowed above a summer garden, red damask roses within and without, likewise the last of the sweet peas and, in the high air, the last of the swifts. Clear soup and a sea-trout shall herald the grouse; iced gooseberry fool shall follow it. We (no dream dinner is without a guest—one guest) shall drink a Burgundy—Corton, I imagine, 1915, a noble and gentle wine, warm as the breath of Juno—and, later (to each a soft thimbleful), a cognac of great dignity and of great age. As for the guest, each man must provide her (*she*, she must surely be?) for himself.[2]

As a footnote to the above it may be said that the flavour of a roast grouse is unsurpassed when it is eaten cold. Remember, though, that a cold grouse should be five minutes underdone, for it will cook while it is cooling. Some cookery books give recipes to be used for either grouse or partridges; this is wrong, for a grouse is a drier bird and will not bear being overdone.

Half a cold grouse is an excellent mainstay of the picnic luncheon basket— compact, easy to eat, delicious and satisfying. I recommend it also for breakfast. When my father and I shared bachelor quarters in London many years ago we looked forward annually to our autumn breakfast grouse. For a salad, Pollard recommended joints of cold grouse with plain lettuce, a touch of fresh tarragon and a cover of stiff mayonnaise sauce. Hard-boiled eggs are admissible but not essential.

A good way of dealing with young grouse, and again it may be eaten hot or cold, is a pie. The recipe of that lovely Edwardian hostess, Georgina, Countess of Dudley, is as follows:

> Take six young grouse and draw them. Cut them in halves and remove the fillets from the bone, reserving the legs. Line a small deep pie dish with slices of streaky bacon and then place in the trails and livers of the grouse and some

chopped chicken livers, also six chopped hard-boiled eggs, some minced parsley and some pieces of very good mushrooms which have been cooked in butter. Place the legs and fillets of grouse in this, then add some of the chopped liver, etc., then more grouse until your dish is full. Add a little very good gravy with a very small quantity of Harvey sauce and pepper and salt. Cover the top with thin slices of bacon. Make a cover with puff paste and, with a paste brush, egg over with one beaten egg. Bake for two hours.[3]

A favourite method of cooking a bird in Edwardian times was the spatchcock. An abbreviation of dispatch cock, this curious term derived from Ireland, was a dish prepared for the unexpected guest and describes vividly the lavishness of Irish hospitality. Lady Dudley's recipe for grouse described by her as a good breakfast or luncheon dish, runs thus:

Pick, draw and singe the bird; split it down the back and cut through the bone; wipe the inside of the bird with a damp cloth; cut off the feet at the first joints; remove the neck close to the body of the bird; flatten and season with salt and pepper; brush over the inside with sweet oil and sprinkle over with finely chopped shallots and parsley; dredge with a little flour; skewer the bird into a flat shape by means of two steel skewers and place it between a well-greased gridiron. Brush over with oiled butter or sweet oil, and cook before, or over, a clear fire (charcoal or gas in preference to a coal fire). Cook from fifteen to twenty minutes, turning the bird occasionally on the gridiron, and baste plentifully from time to time with oiled butter; when done, take the bird from the grill; remove the skewers and dish up with a sharp sauce (Poivrade* or Robert†), or a well-prepared tomato sauce.[4]

If variations on the theme include possibilities for breakfast, lunch and dinner, they include also every course. Minnie, Lady Hindlip, a frequent gourmet guest of my grandparents at Cromlix, had a favourite savoury composed of a stew of dry sherry, espagnole‡ sauce, sultanas, raisins and currants.

---

* Sauce Poivrade: finely diced carrots, onions, celery, a sprig of thyme and crushed bay-leaf are fried in butter until brown. Vinegar and marinade are added, and the whole is cooked for three-quarters of an hour. Ten minutes before straining, a few crushed peppercorns are added.

† Sauce Robert: a finely chopped large onion is gently fried, diluted with white wine and stock and left to simmer for twenty minutes. When dishing up, the sauce is finished with a little mustard.

‡ Sauce espagnole: this is a foundation sauce, and the ingredients may therefore be varied according to taste. A roux of flour and butter is dissolved with brown stock, boiled, and strained two or three times. Tomato purée, diced carrots, onion, celery, turnip, cloves and mushrooms are added. After simmering for an hour it should be finely sieved.

All these dishes are suitable for young birds, but there are plenty of ways to ensure that old birds and those badly damaged by shot are not wasted. But how are we to tell young birds from old? A mature young bird from an early moor on the Twelfth is hard to distinguish from its parents. The only infallible test is to examine the vent and see if there is a bursa or blind pouch just above it. If there is, it is a young bird. However, there are several time-honoured tests which are usually adequate. The third outermost primary wing feather of a young bird is shorter than the rest, and whereas the two outer primaries of an old bird are rounded, the young ones are finer, pointed and more delicate. If the skins of old and young are compared, the old is harsh, the young smooth and soft. The under mandible of the young will not support the weight of the bird when held by it, but breaks at the junction of beak and head. Likewise the skull of a young grouse may be easily crushed with the pressure of a thumb.

One way or another the old and the young may be differentiated. Some gourmets will even say that in taste the Yorkshire grouse which fattens itself on forays to the wheatfields has nothing of the flavour of his Highland cousin. I am no judge of that, but it is true that venison will vary according to whether it has come from a northern forest or a southern park and the Tay salmon is incomparably better than the Tweed. But wherever it comes from, treat a young grouse as a savage and cook it with barbarous simplicity.

The old bird needs ways other than simple roasting:

A souffle may be made by pounding the breasts of two cooked birds in a mortar, with two ounces of fresh butter and a very little core of onion. Rub this through a sieve and add four eggs, the white beaten up to a white froth. Season lightly with salt and add a little cayenne pepper. Bake in a quick oven for twenty minutes. Serve as hot as possible.

Pollard gives a good recipe for soup from old birds:

Three parts cook the bird in the oven. Remove the breast fillets, disjoint, and bray the remainder in a mortar, then add it to a quart or less of good stock which has contained a goodly portion of celery. Fry two oz. of oatmeal with the same amount of butter till a warm brown. Thicken to cream consistency with stock, then add to the stockpot. Let the whole stew or simmer for about an hour and a half.

In the meantime, pound up the fillets and pass them through a sieve to form a meat paste. This can be used to add to the soup in this form, but is preferably made into quenelles with white of egg and 'panada' or flour thickening made by putting one oz. of butter in a pint of boiling salted water and stirring in four oz. of sifted flour. The quenelles made of grouse paste should be small rounds about the size of a teaspoon bowl. These are lightly poached and added to the strained soup, which is now seasoned and should be heated, but not allowed to boil again.

Another form of grouse soup is made by adding grouse carcasses to the familiar Scotch broth of pearl barley, leeks etc. In this case the breast fillets are cut in dice and fried, then added to the soup, whence the carcasses are removed before it comes to the table.[5]

So much for the preparation of grouse, and as we wait to savour it there is, I fear, little to whet our appetite in the feasts of literature. Walter Scott gives it cursory mention when at Ellen's Isle the Knight of Snowdon

> On yonder mountain's purple head
> Have ptarmigan and heathcock bled,[6]

and he endows the cauldron of Meg Merrilies with some savoury contents. '. . . A goodly stew, composed of fowls, hares, partridges and moor game, boiled in a large mess with potatoes, onions and leeks. . . . There's been many a moonlight watch to bring a' that trade thegither . . . the folks that are to eat that dinner thought little o' your game-laws.'[7]

But the most romantic of all tributes lies in an old number of the *Pall Mall Gazette*.

> You come, oh long expected, you are here.
> You come, with joy my eager heart beats high;
> You, vainly longed for nearly half the year,
> So young, so fresh and, oh alas, so dear;
>   Forgive me if I sigh.
>
> Through Spring, through Summer oft have I confessed
> My love for you, from that I've never swerved;
> My menials now shall serve you as 'tis best
>   You should and shall be served.
>
> I have cool recess where you shall wait
> A little while, and shall not wait in vain;

Soon shall you be with me incorporate;
You shall, I swear it, even as elate
   I note that you are twain.

And so my love and joy are plain to see;
My happy paeans echo through the house,
And on next Thursday, Thursday it shall be,
Don't order from the butcher, Jane, for me;
   Since I shall dine on grouse.[8]

MEMORANDA.

Mr Derby 2 to 6 oClock —

Mr Derby Capt Lloyd Capt Pechell &c. 11. to 2

Capt Lloyd . Capt Pechell &c. 12 to 6

Capt Pechell Capt Lloyd & Mr Derby . &c. 11 to 5   (shot a policeman)

Capt Pechell Capt Lloyd   11 to 2

Capt Pechell Mr Aveage 3 to 6

Mr Derby   11 to 5

90 *An 1857 entry in the Cromlix game book. The policeman was entered in the sundries column*

Opposite: *a sketch, dating from 1889, of Cromlix, the author's house in Perthshire*

A Taste of Cromlix

The Cromlix game books comprise a complete record of the shooting since 1856. The plain statistics, brief comments and pen-and-ink sketches by some unknown but talented hand stimulate the imagination more than if the tales these pages could tell were related in their fullness. What, for example, lies behind the casual entry on 12 September 1857, in brackets and without an exclamation mark, 'shot a policeman'? The other items of the bag were four grouse, eighteen patridges and five brown hares; the policeman was entered in the sundries column.

As one turns the pages the changing circumstances of grouse-shooting emerge. In the middle years of the century bags rarely exceeded twenty brace or so and the guns two or three. It was a leisurely business, for it was often noted that only a couple of hours were spent shooting. The laird, Arthur Drummond, would go out with a friend or two, or perhaps the keeper would be instructed to get a few birds for the table or to send away. Sometimes the provider was the family chaplain, the Revd. F. Christmas; he features prominently in the game book and evidently ministered successfully to the bodily as well as to the spiritual needs of the community.

In the 1870s shooting tenants appear, and in 1882 the sport was advertised in Hall's directory *Highland Sportsman*. Driving now began to be practised and one of the tenants was determined to have his money's worth for, in 1884, adjacent to the terse comment 'Mr Burton and many friends' sixteen guns are entered as having participated in the day's sport.

From the game book one learns, too, that in 1880 David Winton came as head keeper. His son, also David, succeeded him, retired in 1953 and retained his association with the estate until his death in 1969. Thus are the centuries spanned and knowledge stored, for if one consulted him on any matter concerning the place he could recall facts from his own experience or from things his father had told him. Nowadays it is unusual for a person to stay in one job more than a few years, and the fragile links that hold together knowledge and tradition snap. This is truer of the life of a rural community than of a town. An industrial or commercial firm can, if it keeps its records over the years, delve into the past and explore preceding events. In the country, much knowledge is of necessity borne in the memory of those that dwell there. The flight of driven grouse in different winds and at different drives, the places where the foxes have their dens, the favourite nesting sites of the hooded crow, the burn that dries up in a drought; these are things that no man can learn quickly.

But if gamekeepers, in common with other professions, change jobs often now-adays, the best of them at least have retained those independent characteristics which endear them to the sportsmen of today as they were endeared to Queen Victoria. There was employed here an underkeeper, Campbell by name, noted for the directness of his remarks. King George of Greece, a not very accurate shot, indicated to Campbell at the end of a drive the fall of a pair of birds. The dogs were put out to retrieve and, to Campbell's surprise, brought back both grouse. 'Yon were twa unlucky birds,' he remarked to the King, whose delight with the remark only equalled his pleasure in the success of his shots. On another occasion Campbell received profuse apology at the end of a drive from a gun who had peppered a beater. 'Never heed,' he was consoled, 'there's aye plenty of them!'

Most things have changed since those days, including the availability of beaters. When estates had a large workforce they were largely self-supporting in terms of beaters, but now it is essential to co-operate with neighbouring estates to ensure that big shooting days do not occur on the same date. Keepers and other workers will pay reciprocal visits to give a helping hand. Additional labour can often be gleaned from the locality by advertisement in the local newspaper, but it can be a dangerous form of assistance in that it attracts some who want to con the ground to embark on a poaching expedition later.

The principal change in forms of grouse-shooting over the past few decades is that pointers and setters are rarely seen now, except in the northern districts of Sutherland, Ross, Caithness and Inverness where huge moors with sparse grouse populations lend themselves particularly to the practice of dogging. This is a sad fact, but the cost of keeping a dog for a year in which it is only going to work for about three weeks is prohibitive.

Driving has not changed at all in the manner it is done, but the cost of beaters and the lack of pointing dogs have made the walking up of grouse a more frequent pastime than it used to be. It has much to recommend it, as any form of walking up game does, from the point of view of healthy exercise, learning about the countryside and, by exploring the contours of the hills, understanding why driven birds fly in particular directions. To some degree pleasure and success will depend on how many birds the moor holds, for not only is it tedious to walk miles and see

91 *Angus MacLauchlan, dog-handler to the late Lady Auckland, the author's mother, with Pride, a Gordon setter, on point*

nothing, but also when birds do rise the shooter is so surprised and unready that they are out of range before the gun is in the shoulder.

One of the blessings of modern life is improved transport. The old fleets of riding and pannier ponies, picturesque though they were, have been superseded by motor vehicles which, tracked or tyred, can convey guns, beaters and all the impedimenta to the very tops of the hills. An essential part of the baggage is, of course, the luncheon basket, and its contents have not changed much over the years. Some egg sandwiches, a few ginger nuts, a piece of shortbread and some fruit was a typical lunch last century and no one would despise that today. What has changed is liquid refreshment, for whereas now a can of beer is the handiest and most popular tipple, a bottle of Apollinaris water was a favourite with the Victorians. It was not so gassy as soda water, and held rather more than the Schweppes bottle. Also, the Polly bottle could be put in a hole and left on the hill whereas the soda water bottle had to be paid for, unless returned. Lastly, the straw envelope of the Polly bottle made a dry seat for those of modest dimensions.

A transient 20th-century custom, at least until the Second World War, was for lunch to be taken alfresco on trestle tables with linen tablecloths. The motor car made this possible, for if the party on the moor was within easy reach of a road at lunch time it was no problem for the chauffeur to take the butler up with all the necessities. The stage was then set for a meal which differed in no way from that which was served ordinarily in the Big House. I recall my grandfather's butler telling me that on one such occasion he forgot the George III cheese scoop and it was a matter of some concern as to how the stilton was going to be served. Now there are no butlers, no chauffeurs and no such lunches.

The keeper has benefited especially from increased mobility. Thirty years ago he was on a bicycle; now he has a Land-Rover or similar vehicle. Without it, considering that the work has to be done by one man where there were perhaps three before the war, the job would be impossible. On many estates the task of the keeper, and of the shepherd and forester, has been eased by the work of Hydro-Electric Boards and the Forestry Commission which have built many roads among the hills. Incidentally, forestry woodlands on the periphery of grouse moors are a nuisance when heather burning is planned; to burn ground adjacent to a forest may be to invite disaster.

Another boon, which has only been brought to many shooting-lodges since the Second World War, is electric light. The paraffin lamps of former times took a man a whole morning to fill and trim, and even if some of them did not smoke, the house was permeated with an unpleasant odour. Enterprising landlords installed electricity generated from petrol or diesel engines, but they had power to produce only light; electric fires were beyond their capacity.

The dress of those who go out to the hill has changed from the colourful costumes of the Victorian era to the uniform estate tweeds of the first part of the century and thence to more drab but practical weatherproof brand-name jackets and trousers of the present day. My grandfather, like many other estate owners,

92 *The author and family party out on the moors*

bought 100 yards of estate tweed each year from Mr Haggart in Aberfeldy, and this was made up into knickerbocker suits for the keepers, foresters and male members of the family as well as coats and skirts for the ladies of the house. Few people can afford such expenditure now.

The modern gun has changed little for a century. The English double-barrel sidelock ejector is still the most prestigious gun in any country, and only among the Italians is the repeater or self-loading gun a favoured weapon. This is in spite of the fact that the earliest repeater, made by Browning, has been in use for over sixty years. George Cornwallis-West told an amusing story in *Edwardian Hey-Days* of one of those novel guns. He arranged a plot with a friend who said to him, when the gun was taken from its corner, 'What a fool you are to come out shooting grouse with a single-barrel gun!'

I was to say nothing, but, at the first point, was to loose off all five barrels as quickly as I could, while he was not to fire at all. We were anxious to see the effect of this performance on the Scottish keepers, who had never even heard of a self-loading gun, let alone seen one. All went beautifully. At the very first point an old cock grouse got up, and I fired off five barrels in about four seconds. The man who was working the dogs fell back in the heather in pure surprise; the other gillies sat down. The head-keeper's remark was: 'Eh gosh! What a terrible weapon!'

The repeater is also unsporting, ugly and cumbersome, as well as being the object of some necessarily harsh remarks on occasion. When foreigners arrive with them we explain that to conform with the custom of the country they must only load with two cartridges. Sometimes they use the language barrier to pretend that they do not understand what we are saying, but they understand readily enough when, after persistently discharging four or five shots at coveys, we say that we are going to pack up and go home. On those sorts of occasion the habitual bluntness of Scottish keepers is an asset in dealing with people who know little about traditional shooting conduct.

Often ignorance stems from the fact that shooting men who were not brought up from childhood trained to the use of a gun by a stern keeper are more numerous than ever. So many people nowadays who have no experience of shooting buy a gun when they are grown up and, no doubt responsible citizens in other ways, they seem incapable of understanding that a gun is a weapon lethal to human beings as well as to birds and animals. The possibility of dangerous shots being fired is therefore a worry, but one thing that may be generally said about modern shooting people is that they do not possess the jealous feelings of past generations. Financial stringency has removed from the scene those professional shots who, beautiful to watch in performance, were quite puerile in their desire to achieve a bigger bag than their neighbour.

If the circus of crack shots who spent the shooting season travelling the country has disappeared, so too have those who entertained them. Few estates with good sporting facilities can afford to forego the income which letting can bring. Letting to a syndicate has long been a customary practice, but in recent years there has been an increasing tendency for shooting to be let on a short-term basis, for two or three days, a week or whatever. The let is often packaged with the sportsmen staying in the lessor's own house, in which because of its size the owner can ill afford to live. In this way useful income can be derived not only to improve the sport but also to maintain the fabric of the house.

The sale of game can also meet a significant part of the costs of the game account. In the days of poor communications little game was sold, and if it came from afar it reached the metropolis in poor condition. To preserve grouse on a journey it was recommended that they should be packed in heather or hops.

(How one was expected to have hops in the north I cannot imagine.) Sometimes dried bladders were used, each holding one bird, and these were sealed up to exclude the air. Any man who could afford not to sell game considered it beneath his dignity to do so, and what he did not consume in his own household was given to friends, tenants, local worthies and institutions such as hospitals. Now, the person who has a full larder of grouse to dispose of on the Twelfth is richly rewarded with an inflated price and high demand from hotels and restaurants. The publicity-seeking restaurateur will employ aeroplane, helicopter and bag-piper to bring the little bird from the moor to the dining table, and if he is fortunate the news media will give him free advertisement.

At Cromlix we optimise our income from shooting in any way we can, and as hosts to many different nationalities we find the manifestation of different national characteristics interesting. The Belgians seem to do the sporting circuit of the globe and delight as much in killing a blue hare as a grouse. The French, charming and generous, derive huge enjoyment from their sport and laugh away good humouredly the rebukes of the keeper when their enthusiasm overruns. The Finns, most correct in their approach, are imbued with an old-fashioned courtesy and incline to be a little put out if their marksmanship errs. The Italians, bubbling over with enjoyment of everything, are full of bonhomie, unamenable to disci-pline not only on the moor but in the house. Some of them bring supplies of their own native food which they like to prepare themselves and share with us; with cries of 'I make you nice pasta' they invade the kitchen, to the consternation of the cook.

The British, happy to relate, are the most sportsmanlike of all, resigned to the intermittent day ruined with mist or heavy rain or by a hen harrier quartering the ground and thereby dispersing the birds in all directions except over the guns. Rarely do they grudge not getting what others might have considered their money's worth.

On the matter of foreigners, a word of warning to anyone who may be letting his shooting to people of different races: never mix the nationalities. Although the draw for places may be as fair a system as can be devised, from time to time there will be a drama in which either it is inferred that the organisation of the shoot has favoured one nation against another or, perhaps, a neighbour gun of different nationality will be charged with extending the arc of his fire to include birds which territorially should not be his. Diplomatic oil has to be poured on the situation to restore equanimity, but already the day's sport will have been marred.

The moor owner's estate account will also be marred if he does not take steps to ensure that he gets payment for the sport and services he provides, including a cancellation fee if his clients fail to arrive. Hence he is wise in all cases, except where the sportsmen are trusted friends, to employ a sporting agent to act for him. The agent's fee is well earned; the work may involve not only finding clients in the first place but also arranging their travel, gun licences and other time-consuming details which would be a nuisance to the lessor if he tried to cope with them himself.

There are worries enough anyway in the months preceding the Twelfth, apart from anxiety on the day of a shoot. It is always impossible to know even approximately how many days to plan in advance; not only may the breeding season be disastrous but even if it is successful the earlier shooting parties may be such crack shots that there may not be enough birds for the later parties. Spring weather is a prime factor in the difference between success and failure. At least one can do nothing about it and one worries therefore the less, but vermin is another matter. The keeper, gloomy by nature, for that way he can smile and make his employer smile when his pessimism is disproved, paints dramatic pictures of doom. Droves of carrion or hooded crows from some unkeepered neighbour will be sweeping the moor and gobbling up all the eggs. Black-backed gulls flock in from everywhere, and as for the marks of foxes emanating from the deer forest in the north, well, quite clearly the keeper there is doing nothing about them. A nightmare vision is conjured up of predators in the air and on the ground that will leave the hills barren of game.

Most years at Cromlix everything turns out all right, and if tactics do go wrong sometimes or the weather ruins a day, at least the scene we have set is right and that is at least as essential as the provision of good sport.

General Garamie, in his chair by the fire, checked and rechecked his meticulous arrangements for the morrow: map, horn, whistle, extractor, guns, cartridges, drives, beaters, flankers, loaders, dogs, luncheon, drinks, ice, game-labels and trains; for to him a day's grouse-driving needed from start to finish the most careful 'operation orders'. (J. K. Stanford, *The Twelfth*, p. 50.)

If the day is clear the sheer joy of being on the hill is a holiday in itself. As he awaits the coming of the drive the shooter has leisure to survey the scene around him. A group of deer, disturbed by the beaters, may come past and if he is exceptionally fortunate an eagle will sail over from Glenartney. Apart from the soaring larks and the wind in the heather there is little sound, though he can spy from his vantage point the great centres of industry. In the valley below, Stirling

Castle stands guard over the passes to the north, and in the distant haze beyond lie Falkirk and Grangemouth. The eye moves westward along the horizon of hills, The Cobbler, Ben Lomond, Ben Ledi, all snow-capped if this is late autumn. 'Coming on your right,' calls the warning voice of the next gun, and attention is directed to the approaching covey, skimming low, difficult to detect against the similarly coloured backcloth of peat and heather.

When the day is over, and feet are up at the fire, whatever disappointments may have been suffered can be forgotten in the creature comforts of a vanished world. To inherit an enormous Victorian mansion is, most would say, a mixed blessing, but we have had a lot of pleasure from it and we believe that we have given a lot of pleasure also. Characteristically, the house was added to at the end of the last century when landowners were competing with one another to build bigger and better. Better, that is, not so much in architectural style as in quality of material and of material comfort. From the outside it is eccentric, rather like a barrack, without much sense of design; inside the rooms are beautiful and of noble proportions without being baronial. When we came to live in it in 1971, three previous generations had lived in it since it was built in 1875. Little had been changed over the years, and much turning out needed to be done. But we were careful to preserve the best features of the decor and furnishings, and through my wife's genius as an interior decorator the character of a large Victorian shooting-lodge has been retained. Every house has an atmosphere, good, bad or indifferent. Ours is friendly but sad when there are few people in it; when it is full it springs to life, revelling in company, sharing in the laughter, emitting warmth.

On the last evening of our guests' visit we retire to the library after dinner and enter up the game book.

The party all knew each other well and had by now exchanged most of their grouse-shooting shop at dinner: 'Poor Gerald, yes, he's had a most indifferent hatch, a lot of eggs frozen, and the heather beetle's been worrying him since . . . Let me see, who *has* got Morven this year, oh yes, some Americans at a quite staggering figure, considering the stock Tom left there. . . . Yes, we had quite a pretty little week at Crashie last September, not a petticoat in the lodge. . . . Fourth time over, but they always seem to have birds there . . . are you? I'm going to the Duke on the 19th . . . oh, average year only, he tells me . . . poor old Snooper, he was always a bit of a boy-scout at m'tutor's, but now he's gone all romantic and taken a dogging moor in Kintyre . . . Jimmy Smitherman told me it's the sort of place where you walk twenty-five miles a day for $2\frac{1}{2}$ brace . . . a very fair little hatch, he assures me, and he's taken on the Dalziel beat from

The MacMurtrie, which rounds him off very nicely. . . . *Strongylosis* my foot! it's his keeper! He *will* not burn and he doesn't know the first thing about a moor!' (J. K. Stanford, *The Twelfth*, p. 49.)

Then we turn over the pages of the old game books, and many of our friends who are here for the first time are excited to find that their grandfathers came here to shoot a hundred years ago. Let us hope that in the next century their descendants will be able to look back likewise, and that changes in the country scene will not have been too drastic.

Upon the hills at least, the immemorial pattern of life is likely to continue, and with it the way of the grouse. The rearing of grouse has never been carried out successfully on any scale, because they do not have the ability to adjust from an artificial diet to their natural heather diet. For this we must be thankful, for if they could be reared as pheasants the magic and romance would vanish. It is ironic, therefore, that a bird which flourishes on ground that provides only relatively poor grazing for domestic animals; which yields a significant food supply; whose management is consistent with good husbandry and ecological stability of habitat; and which brings to Britain valuable currency from overseas sportsmen, has generated a hackneyed term of derision and contempt beloved of the radicals. The grouse moor image! Why not the pheasant covert image or the golf course image? For all the sting the term is intended to carry across the debating chamber or from the orator's platform, I believe that when a Premier retired in the autumn recess to Bolton Abbey or The Hirsel, the people at large derived a certain measure of reassurance. The leader of the nation was on the high moors, the nation was secure and each and every citizen could take their holiday and go about their particular pleasures with contentment.

93 *Archibald Thorburn*, The Last Before Dark

Sources

I EARLIEST TIMES

2 A Sporting Resort
1. Augustus Hare, *Story of My Life*, vol. II.
2. Elizabeth Longford, *Wellington: Pillar of State*, Panther Books edn., p. 99.
3. Violet Dickinson (ed.), *Miss Eden's Letters*, p. 104.
4. Dickinson (ed.), op. cit., p. 182.

II DELIGHTS EXPECTED

3 Taking a Moor
1. Anthony Trollope, *The Duke's Children*, Panther Books edn., p. 280.
2. Eric Parker (ed.), *The Shooting Week-End Book*, p. 279.
3. J. D. Carrick (ed.), *The Laird of Logan*, p. 54.

4 The Journey North
1. Herbert Byng Hall, *Highland Sports and Highland Quarters*, vol. II, p. 117.
2. *Badminton Magazine*, July/December 1897, p. 615.
3. Lord Malmesbury, *Memoirs of an Ex-Minister*.
4. Ernest Briggs, *Angling and Art in Scotland*, p. 89.
5. Fores's *Sporting Notes and Sketches*, vol. IV, p. 96.

5 Highland Quarters
1. Malmesbury, op. cit., vol. III, p. 73.
2. Sir Walter Scott, *St Ronan's Well* (vol. VIII of 1845 edn. of the 'Waverley' Novels), p. 341.
3. Osgood MacKenzie, *A Hundred Years in the Highlands*, p. 173.
4. Byng Hall, op. cit., vol. I, p. 60.
5. Trollope, op. cit., p. 283.

III THE CHASE

6 The Noble Grouse
1. See J. G. Millais, *The Natural History of British Game Birds*, pp. 38–43.

7 Dogs
1. MacKenzie, op. cit., p. 115 et seq.
2. Charles St John, *Tour in Sutherland*, vol. I, p. 279.
3. Harding Cox and Gerald Lascelles, *Coursing and Falconry*, pp. 248–50.

8 Driving
1. Abel Chapman, *Memories of Fourscore Years Less Two*, p. 197.
2. Sir John Astley, *Fifty Years of My Life*, vol. II, p. 253.
3. A. Grimble, *Shooting and Salmon Fishing*, p. 83.
4. Lord Granville Gordon, *Sporting Reminiscences*, p. 115.
5. Patrick Chalmers, *The Frequent Gun*, p. 143.

IV THE SEASON

9 August
1. Anthony Trollope, *The Eustace Diamonds*, pp. 329–31.

10 Ladies!
1. A. Grimble, *Highland Sport*, p. 24.
2. Astley, op. cit., vol. II, p. 264.
3. Mrs A. Tweedie, *Wilton Q.C. or Life in a Highland Shooting Box*, p. 106.
4. Astley, op. cit., vol. II, p. 265.
5. Byng Hall, op. cit., vol. II, p. 109.
6. E. MacKenzie, *In Grouseland*, p. 245.

11 Bye Days
1. Fores's *Sporting Notes and Sketches*, 1898, p. 272.
2. Innes Shand, *Shooting*, p. 115.
3. Hesketh Prichard, *Sport in Wildest Britain*, p. 209.
4. Fur, Feather and Fin Series, *The Trout*, p. 57.
5. Queen Victoria, *Leaves from the Journal of Our Life in the Highlands*, p. 125.
6. Elizabeth Grant, *Memoirs of a Highland Lady 1797–1827*, p. 204.

V ARTS OF THE MOOR

12 Painters in the Heather
1. J. G. Millais, *The Life and Letters of Sir John Everett Millais*, vol. II, p. 61.
2. G. E. Lodge, *Memoirs of an Artist Naturalist*, p. 84.

13 Fireside Tales
1. See the Memoir of Charles St John by Cosmo Innes in *Natural History and Sport in Moray*.
2. Charles St John, *Wild Sports and Natural History of the Highlands*, p. 30.
3. A. E. Gathorne-Hardy, *Autumns in Argyleshire*, p. 188.
4. A. J. Stuart-Wortley, 'Shooting the Grouse', in Fur and Feather Series, *The Grouse*, p. 85.
5. Stuart-Wortley, op. cit., p. 96.
6. Ibid.
7. First published in *Green Days and Blue Days* and subsequently in *The Lonsdale Anthology of Sporting Prose and Verse*, p. 55.

14 Dining on Grouse

1. H. B. C. Pollard, *The Sportsman's Cookery Book*, pp. 24–5.
2. Patrick Chalmers, *The Shooting-Man's England*, p. 217.
3. Georgina, Countess of Dudley, *The Dudley Book of Cookery and Household Recipes*, p. 75.
4. Georgina, Countess of Dudley, *A Second Dudley Book of Cookery and Other Recipes*, p. 101.
5. Pollard, op. cit., p. 25.
6. Sir Walter Scott, 'The Lady of the Lake', canto I, stanza XXII, *Poetical Works*, O.U.P. edn., 1966.
7. Sir Walter Scott, *Guy Mannering*, Robert Cadell edn., 1842, pp. 609–10.
8. Requoted from Patrick Chalmers, *At the Sign of the Dog and Gun*, p. 11.

Bibliography

Abbott, S., *Ardenmohr among the Hills*, Chapman & Hall, London, 1876.
Adams, W. A., *Twenty-Six Years Reminiscences of Scotch Grouse Moors*, Horace Cox, London, 1889.
Aflalo, F. G. (ed.), *The Cost of Sport*, John Murray, London, 1899.
Arkwright, W., *The Pointer and his Predecessors*, Arthur L. Humphreys, London, 1902.
Ash, E. C., *This Doggie Business*, Hutchinson, London, 1934.
Astley, Sir John, *Fifty Years of My Life*, Hurst & Blackett, London, 1894.

Badminton Magazine of Sports and Pastimes, Longmans Green, London.
Bannerman, D. A., and Lodge, G. E., *The Birds of the British Isles*, vol. XII, Oliver & Boyd, Edinburgh, 1963.
Barbier, C. P., *Samuel Rogers and William Gilpin*, O.U.P., London, for Glasgow University, 1959.
Birch Reynardson, C. T. S., *Down the Road, or Reminiscences of a Gentleman Coachman*, Longmans Green, London, 1875.
Black, W., *White Wings*, Macmillan, London, 1880.
Blaine, D. P., *An Encyclopaedia of Rural Sports*, Longman, Brown, Green & Longmans, London, 1852.
Boswell, J., *The Journal of a Tour to the Hebrides*, ed. R. W. Chapman, O.U.P., London, 1924.
Bovill, E. W., *English Country Life 1780–1830*, O.U.P., London, 1962.
Breadalbane, Marchioness of, *The High Tops of Black Mount*, William Blackwood, Edinburgh and London, 1907.
Bromley-Davenport, W., *Sport*, Chapman & Hall, London, 1885.
Brown, Ivor, *Balmoral*, Collins, London, 1955.
Burt, E., *Letters from a Gentleman in the North of Scotland*, London, 1815.

Cameron, A. E. et al., *The Heather Beetle*, British Field Sports Society, Petworth, n.d.
Cameron, A. G., *The Wild Red Deer of Scotland*, William Blackwood, Edinburgh and London, 1923.
Campbell, R. H., *Scotland since 1707*, Basil Blackwell, Oxford, 1971.
    and Dow, J. B. A., *Source Book of Scottish Economic and Social History*, Basil Blackwell, Oxford, 1968.
Carrick, J. D. (ed.), *The Laird of Logan*, Robert Forrester, Glasgow, 1878.
Carruthers, R., *The Highland Note-Book*, Courier Office, Inverness, 1887.
Carswell, D., *Sir Walter*, John Murray, London, 1932.
Cazenove, B., *Grouse Shooting and Moor Management*, Country Life, London, 1936.
Chalmers, P. R., *The Frequent Gun and a Little Fishing*, Philip Allan, London, 1928.
    At the Sign of the Dog and Gun, Philip Allan, London, 1930.
    Mine Eyes to the Hills: An Anthology of the Highland Forest, A. & C. Black, London, 1931.
    The Shooting-Man's England, Seeley Service, London, n.d.
Chapman, A., *Memories of Fourscore Years Less Two, 1851–1929*, Gurney & Jackson, London, 1930.

Lord Chesterfield, *Letters to His Son and Others*, J. M. Dent, London, 1951.

Coats, R. H., *Travellers' Tales of Scotland*, Alexander Gardner, Paisley, 1913.

Coles, C. (ed.), *The Complete Book of Game Conservation*, Barrie & Jenkins, London, 1971.

Colquhoun, J., *The Moor and The Loch*, William Blackwood, Edinburgh and London, 1840.

Committee of Inquiry on Grouse Disease, *The Grouse in Health and in Disease*, Smith Elder, London, 1911.

Cornwallis-West, G., *Edwardian Hey-Days*, Putnam, London and New York, 1930.

Cox, Harding, and Lascelles, G., *Coursing and Falconry*, Longmans Green, London, 1892.

Cuming, E. D., *British Sport Past and Present*, Hodder & Stoughton, London, 1909.
  Covert and Field Sport, Hodder & Stoughton, London, n.d.

Cunnington, P., and Mansfield, A., *English Costume for Sports and Outdoor Recreation*, A. & C. Black, London, 1969.

Cupples, G., *Scotch Deer-Hounds and their Masters*, William Blackwood, Edinburgh and London, 1894.

Cutcliffe-Hyne, C. J., *Ben Watson*, Country Life, London, 1926.

Daniel, The Revd. W. B., *Rural Sports*, Longman, Hurst, Rees & Orme, London, 1807.

Day, J. W., *The Dog in Sport*, G. G. Harrap, London, 1938.

Dudley, Georgina Countess of, *The Dudley Book of Cookery and Household Recipes*, Edward Arnold, London, 1913.
  A Second Dudley Book of Cookery and Other Recipes, Hutchinson, London, 1914.

Eden, Emily, *Miss Eden's Letters*, ed. Violet Dickinson, Macmillan, London, 1919.

Edwards, L., *My Scottish Sketch Book*, Country Life, London, 1929.

Egan, Pierce, *Sporting Anecdotes*, Sherwood Jones, London, 1825.

Ensor, R. C. K., *England 1870–1914*, Clarendon Press, Oxford, 1952.

Fores's *Sporting Notes and Sketches*, vols. I–XXI, Fores, London, 1885–1904.

Fraser Darling, F., and Boyd, J. M., *The Highlands and Islands*, Collins, London, 1964.

Galt, J., *Annals of the Parish*, T. N. Foulis, Edinburgh and London, 1919.
  The Last of the Lairds, Foulis, London, 1926.

Gaskell, P., *Morvern Transformed*, C.U.P., Cambridge, 1968.

Gathorne-Hardy, A. E., *Autumns in Argyleshire*, Longmans Green, London, 1900.
  My Happy Hunting Grounds, Longmans Green, London, 1914.

Geikie, Sir Archibald, *Scottish Reminiscences*, James Maclehose, Glasgow, 1904.

Gibbon, E., *Autobiography*, O.U.P., London, 1950.

Gordon, Lord Granville, *Sporting Reminiscences*, Grant Richards, London, 1902.

Graham, H. G., *The Social Life of Scotland in the Eighteenth Century*, A. & C. Black, London, 1900.

Grant, Elizabeth, of Rothiemurchus, *Memoirs of a Highland Lady 1797–1827*, John Murray, London, 1960.

Grant, I. F., *Highland Folk Ways*, Routledge & Kegan Paul, London, 1961.

Greener, W. W., *The Gun and its Development*, Cassell, London, 8th edn., 1907.

Grimble, A., *Deer-Stalking*, Chapman & Hall, London, 1888.
  Shooting and Salmon Fishing, Chapman & Hall, London, 1892.
  Highland Sport, Chapman & Hall, London, 1894.

The Deer Forests of Scotland, Kegan Paul, Trench, Trübner, London, 1896.
Leaves From a Game Book, Kegan Paul, Trench, Trübner, London, 1898.
The Salmon Rivers of Scotland, Kegan Paul, Trench, Trübner, London, 1902.
More Leaves From My Game Book, R. Clay, London, 1917.

Haldane, A. R. B., *New Ways Through the Glens*, Thomas Nelson, Edinburgh, 1962.
Haldane, Elizabeth S., *The Scotland of Our Fathers*, Alexander Maclehose, London, 1933.
Hall, H. B., *Highland Sports and Highland Quarters*, H. Hurst, London, n.d.
Hartley, G. W., *Wild Sport With Gun, Rifle and Salmon-Rod*, William Blackwood, Edinburgh and London, 1903.
Wild Sport and Some Stories, William Blackwood, Edinburgh and London, 1912.
Hawker, Lt.-Col. P., *Instructions to Young Sportsmen in all that relates to Guns and Shooting*, Herbert Jenkins, London, 1922. (1st edn., 1814.)
Hesketh Prichard, H., *Sport in Wildest Britain*, Philip Allan, London, n.d.
Minnie, Lady Hindlip, *Minnie Lady Hindlip's Cookery Book*, Thornton Butterworth, London, 1925.
Hume Brown, P., *Early Travellers in Scotland*, David Douglas, Edinburgh, 1891.
Hutchinson, H. G. (ed.), *Shooting*, Country Life, London, 1903.
Hutchinson, General W. N., *Dog Breaking*, John Murray, London, 6th edn., 1876.

'Idstone', *The 'Idstone' Papers*, Horace Cox, London, 1872.
Irvine, A. F., *Treatise on the Game Laws of Scotland*, T. & T. Clark, Edinburgh, 1883.

Jeans, T., *The Tommiebeg Shootings*, George Routledge, London, n.d.
Johnson, Dr Samuel, *A Journey to the Western Isles*, ed. E. W. Chapman, O.U.P., London, 1924.
Johnson, T. B., *The Shooter's Companion*, Edwards & Knibb, London

Lennox, Lord William, *Pictures of Sporting Life and Character*, Hurst & Blackett, London, 1860.
Lettice, J., *Letters on a Tour Through Various Parts of Scotland in the year 1792*, T. Cadell, London, 1794.
Lodge, G. E., *Memoirs of an Artist Naturalist*, Gurney & Jackson, London and Edinburgh, 1946.
Longford, Elizabeth, *Victoria R.I.*, Weidenfeld & Nicolson, London, 1964.

Macaulay, Lord, *The History of England*, Crosby, Nichols, Lee, Boston, 1861.
McCausland, H., *Old Sporting*, Batchworth Press, London, 1948.
MacDonald, D. G. F., *Cattle, Sheep and Deer*, Steel & Jones, London, 1872.
MacKenzie of Inverewe, O. H., *A Hundred Years in the Highlands*, Geoffrey Bles, London, 1974. (1st edn., 1921.)
Malcolm, G., and Maxwell, A., *Grouse and Grouse Moors*, A. & C. Black, London, 1910.
Malmesbury, Earl of, *Memoirs of an Ex-Minister*, Bernhard Tauchnitz, Leipzig, 1885.
Margetson, S., *Journey by Stages*, Cassell, London, 1967.
'Martingale', *Sporting Scenes and Country Characters*, Longman, Orme, Brown Green & Longmans, London, 1840.
Millais, J. G., *The Life and Letters of Sir John Everett Millais*, Methuen, London, 1899.
The Natural History of British Game Birds, Longmans Green, London, 1909.

Minto, Nina Countess of, *Letters and Journals*, ed. Hon. A. D. Elliot, privately printed 1920.

Nevill, R., *Sporting Days and Sporting Ways*, Duckworth, London, 1910.
    The Man of Pleasure, Chatto & Windus, London, 1912.
    Old English Sporting Prints and Their History, The Studio, London, 1923.
    Old English Sporting Books, The Studio, London, 1924.
'Nimrod', *The Chase, the Turf and the Road*, John Murray, London, 1870.
Noakes, A., *The World of Henry Alken*, Witherby, London, 1952.
Notestein, W., *The Scot in History*, Jonathan Cape, London, 1946.

Oakleigh, T., *The Oakleigh Shooting Code*, James Ridgway, London, 1837.
Ogilvie-Grant, W. R. et al., *British Game Birds and Wildfowl* (vol. 1 of *The Gun at Home and Abroad*), The London and Counties Press Association, London, 1912.

Parker, E. (ed.), *The Lonsdale Keeper's Book*, Seeley Service, London, n.d.
    The Lonsdale Anthology of Sporting Prose and Verse, Seeley Service, London, 1932.
    Shooting by Moor, Field and Shore, Seeley Service, London, n.d.
Payne-Gallwey, Sir Ralph, *Letters to Young Shooters*, Longmans Green, London, 1890.
Peel, C. V. A., *Wild Sport in the Outer Hebrides*, F. E. Robinson, London, 1901.
Peel, E. L., *A Highland Gathering*, Longmans Green, London, 1885.
Pennant, Thomas, *A Tour in Scotland*, John Monk, Chester, 1774.
Pollard, H. B. C., *A History of Firearms*, Geoffrey Bles, London, 1926.
    The Sportsman's Cookery Book, Country Life, London, 1926.
    Game Birds, Eyre & Spottiswoode, London, 1929.
    The Gun Room Guide, Eyre & Spottiswoode, London, 1930.
Punch Library of Humour, Educational Book Co., London, n.d.

Ramsay, Dean, *Reminiscences of Scottish Life and Character*, T. N. Foulis, Edinburgh, n.d.
Rawstorne, L., *Gamonia*, Methuen, London, 1905. (1st edn., 1837.)
Rogers, H. C. B., *Turnpike to Iron Road*, Seeley Service, London, 1961.

Scott, Lord George, *Grouse Land and the Fringe of the Moor*, Witherby, London, 1937.
Scott, Sir Walter, *Waverley Novels*.
Scrope, W., *The Art of Deer Stalking*, John Murray, London, 1838.
Shand, A. I., *Mountain Stream and Covert*, Seeley, London, 1897.
    Shooting, J. M. Dent, London, 1902.
Shaw Sparrow, W., *British Sporting Artists*, John Lane The Bodley Head, London, 1922.
    A Book of Sporting Painters, John Lane The Bodley Head, London, 1931.
Smollett, T., *The Expedition of Humphry Clinker*, Folio Society edn., London, 1955.
Speedy, T., *Sport in the Highlands and Lowlands of Scotland*, William Blackwood, Edinburgh and London, 1884.
Sporting Magazine.
'The Sportsman' (ed.), *British Sports and Sportsmen*, British Sports and Sportsmen, London, 1913.
Spottiswoode, J., *The Moorland Gamekeeper*, David & Charles, Newton Abbot, 1977.
Stanford, J. K., *The Twelfth*, Faber & Faber, London, 1944.
    Grouse Shooting, Percival Marshall, London, 1963.

Stephens, M., *Grouse Shooting*, A. & C. Black, London, 1939.
'Stonehenge', *Manual of British Rural Sports*, G. Routledge, London, 1856.
St John, C., *Sketches of the Wild Sports and Natural History of the Highlands*, John Murray, London, 1845.
　A Tour in Sutherlandshire, John Murray, London, 1849.
　Natural History and Sport in Moray, David Douglas, Edinburgh, 1882.
　Note Books 1846–1853, David Douglas, Edinburgh, 1901.

Tait, J. H., *A Treatise on the Law of Scotland as applied to the game laws, trout and salmon fishing*, William Green, Edinburgh, 1901.
Thomas, J., *The West Highland Railway*, Pan Books, London, 1970.
Thompson, F. M. L., *English Landed Society in the Nineteenth Century*, Routledge & Kegan Paul, London, 1963.
Thomson, D., *England in the Nineteenth Century*, Penguin Books, Harmondsworth, 1951.
Thorburn, A., *Game Birds and Wild-Fowl of Great Britain and Ireland*, Longmans Green, London, 1923.
Thornhill, R. B., *The Shooting Directory*, Longman, Hurst, Rees & Orme, London, 1804.
Trevelyan, G. M., *English Social History*, Longmans Green, London, 1942.
Trollope, Anthony, *Phineas Finn*, Panther Books edn., St Albans, 1973.
　The Eustace Diamonds, Penguin Books edn., Harmondsworth, 1973.
　The Duke's Children, Panther Books edn., St Albans, 1973.
Tweedle, Mrs Alec, *Wilton Q.C. or Life in a Highland Shooting Box*, Horace Cox, London, 1895.

Vallance, H. A., *The Highland Railway*, David & Charles, Newton Abbot, 3rd edn., 1969.
Queen Victoria, *Leaves from the Journal of Our Life in the Highlands*, Smith Elder, London, 1868; Folio Society, London, 1973.

Wallace, H. F., *Happier Years*, Eyre & Spottiswoode, London, 1944.
　Hunting Winds, Eyre & Spottiswoode, London, 1949.
　Please Ring the Bell, Eyre & Spottiswoode, London, 1952.
Walsingham, Lord, and Sir Ralph Payne-Gallway, *Shooting: Moor and Marsh*, Longmans Green, London, 2nd edn., 1887.
Watson, A. E. T., *King Edward VII as a Sportsman*, Longmans Green, London, 1911.
Watson, J. S., *The Reign of George III*, Clarendon Press, Oxford, 1960.
Wilson, Prof. J., ('Christopher North'), *Noctes Ambrosianae*, Hamilton Adams, London, 1888.
Woodward, E. L., *The Age of Reform*, Clarendon Press, Oxford, 1939.

Index

Page numbers in italics indicate illustrations

landlords, landowners, 32; oppose railways, 55; and holiday accommodation, 68, 69; prestigious mansions, 69; and game preservation, 177

Landseer, Sir Edwin, 69, 162

Lascelles, G., and Cox, Harding, on grouse-hawking, 97–9

Leech, John, 162, 171; creator of Mr Briggs, 157

Leith, 16, 51, 177

Leven, River, *148*, *149*

Leveson-Gower, Lady Francis, at Dunrobin, 121

Levidis, Major, *129*

Lilford, Thomas Powys, 4th Baron, *British Birds*, 163, 170

ling heather (*Calluna vulgaris*), 74, 78–9, 81; *74*

loaders, 115, 116

Loch Einich, 23

Loch Katrine, 17

Loch Leven, 20; *148*, *149*

Loch Lomond, 17

Loch Maree, 92

Loch Tay, 20

Loch Torridon–Loch Broom highway, 52

Lochnagar, *33*

Lockhart, John Gibson, and Melrose Abbey (*Life of Scott*), 16

Lodge, George E., painter-sportsman, 20, 161

lodges, *see* shooting-boxes

London–Scotland, coach and rail services, 50, 53, 55

London life, and grouse-shooting, 31; absentee Scottish landlords, 37, 54; and the railway, 55–6; hansom cabs and cabbies, 56; eating houses, 179

Lovat, Lord, 73

Lowlands, by coach northwards, 53–4

Macaulay, Thomas Babington, Lord, 49

MacBrayne, steamer owner, 51

McIntyre & Stewart, Perth bakers, 60

McKellar, Rab, anecdote, 44

McKendrick, William, butcher, 60

Mackenzie's of Dingwall, *66*

MacKenzie, Evan, 46–7; *Grouse Shooting*, 93; *In Grouseland*, 139

MacKenzie, Dr John, *Highland Memories*, 172

MacKenzie, Osgood, *A Hundred Years in the Highlands*, 64, 91–2, 172; retrievers: Shot, 91–2, Fan, 92–3

MacKintosh of Moy, pioneer of driving, 109

MacLauchlan, Angus, dog-handler, *189*

McPhail, Rodger, 166; *165*

MacPherson, H. A., and Stuart-Wortley, A., *The Grouse*, 170–1

Malcolm, G., and Maxwell, A., *Grouse and Grouse Moors*, 102

Malmesbury, Lord, 53, 63, 150; cost of sporting rights, 39

Mannock Moors, *109*

Manton, Joseph, gunsmith, 22, 28, 32

Mar, Lord, 32, 151

Mar Lodge, *42*, *62*

Maxwell, Sir Herbert, 20

Mazarin, Auguste, cook to Millais, 160

Mealbannock shooting-lodge, 141

Mendips, the, 77

Methven Simpson, pianos for shooting-lodges, 126

Milbank, Sir Frederick, record killing at Wemmergill, 114–15

Millais, Sir John, painting sportsman, 157–61; the Laird in *Trilby*, 160

Millais, J. G., 83, 158; works on *British Game Birds*, 78, 140, 161

Minto, Nina, Countess of, on moorland sport, 137–8

Monk, General, deforests Aberfoyle, 37

moorland fauna, 141–3

Moray Firth, 77

Morgan, M. S., salmon fishing, *145*

Morris, William, shooting anecdote, 110–11

motor vehicles, aids to shooting, 70, 189–90

Mr Punch in the Highlands, *115*, *133*, *134*, *138*, *171*

Murray, Hilda, of Elibank, *135*; *Echoes of Sport*, 137

Murthly Castle, 158, 160

Nature Conservancy Research Station, Banchory, 74

Neale, Edward, *86*

Nicholson, E. W., at Dunrobin, 126

North, Christopher (John Wilson), 95

Northcote, Sir Stafford, 150

Oakleigh, Thomas, *Shooting Code*, 40–1, 63

Ophelia, HMS, covey of grouse, 77